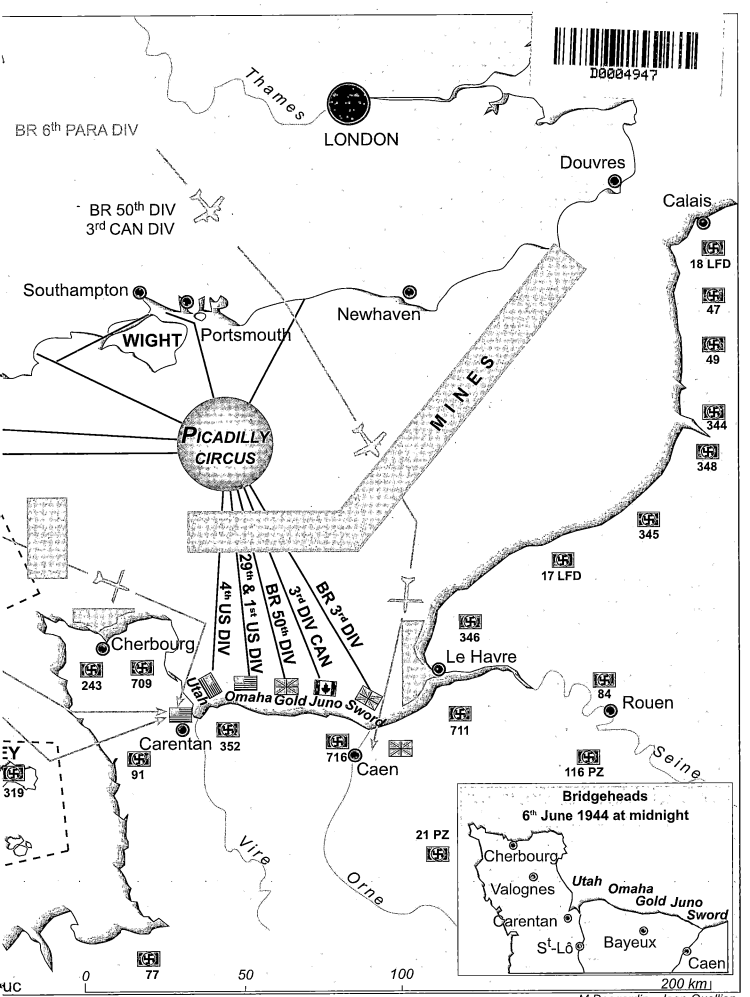

BR 6th PARA DIV

BR 50th DIV
3rd CAN DIV

Thames

LONDON

Douvres

Calais

18 LFD

47

49

344

348

Southampton

Newhaven

WIGHT Portsmouth

PICADILLY CIRCUS

MINES

345

17 LFD

346

Le Havre

84 Rouen

4th US DIV

29th & 1st US DIV

BR 50th DIV

3rd DIV CAN

BR 3rd DIV

Cherbourg

243 709

Utah

Omaha Gold Juno Sword

Carentan 352

91

716 Caen

711

Seine

Y

319

Vire

Orne

21 PZ

116 PZ

Bridgeheads
6th June 1944 at midnight

Cherbourg

Valognes *Utah Omaha*

Gold Juno

Carentan *Sword*

St-Lô Bayeux

Caen

0   50   100

77

200 km

UC

M.Desgardin - Jean-Quellien

NORMANDY 44

Jean Quellien

Professor of Contemporary History at Caen University,
Second World War specialist, and prolific author.
Other Memorial / Ouest-France publications include :
La Normandie au cœur de la guerre
Histoire de la Seconde Guerre mondiale, 1939-1945

Translation by John Ritchie

Le Mémorial de Caen
UN MUSÉE POUR LA PAIX

Éditions Mémorial de Caen - Espl. Eisenhower - 14000 Caen - France
Tél. : +33 (0)2 31 06 06 44

THE LONGEST NIGHT

"In spite of the scattered nature of the landings, the airborne divisions completed their missions. They managed to take the enemy by surprise and caused considerable confusion, disrupting his communications and disorganising his defences."

*General Montgomery,
Commander of the 21ˢᵗ Army Group.*

THE END OF THE NIGHTMARE?

Caen, 5th June 1944. Midnight was fast approaching. The town's lights were out, due to the curfew, but the town was not asleep. The muffled thud of explosions could be distinctly heard coming from the coast, 10 miles away. One or two fortunate people in the more elevated parts of the town, who had climbed up to their attics, could make out the distant horizon, lit by the glow of a fantastic conflagration. The ground was trembling, windows vibrating. At first people thought the Allies were bombarding the Atlantic Wall again. During the preceding weeks the attacks on the German fortifications had multiplied, but this time, they were lasting longer than usual. Was this the invasion?

The invasion! Each and every one had dreamed about it for several months, and it was the main topic of every conversation. It had been expected in spring and awaited in summer 1943, but in vain. Had Churchill not announced that it would happen before the autumn leaves fell? But the leaves had fallen and nothing had happened; German propaganda had been heavily ironic. With the passing of winter, the return of spring gave new hope to the French, as it did to all the peoples of Western Europe, who had been living under the Nazi jackboot for four long years.

Four long years of nightmare, consisting of the sound of jackboots echoing on the cobblestones, banners bearing the swastika flying over the steps leading up to public buildings, privations, prohibition, humiliation and fear. Marshal Goering, in charge of the political economy of the occupied territories, had made his position clear: *"I intend to pillage and to pillage abundantly."* He did not exercise moderation. Whole convoys of cattle,

corn, wine, coal and quantities of other products requisitioned by the victors were sent to Germany, leaving the population, and in particular those living in cities, to the agony of a daily life consisting of shortages of all kinds, the problems of rationing, endless queuing at shop doors, gnawing hunger and the merciless cold of winter. Many had no option but barter and the black market if they wanted to survive.

For many women and children, the war was synonymous with a long drawn out separation from their husbands and fathers, prisoners somewhere on the other side of the Rhine. From 1942 onwards, and because it was short of manpower for its colossal war effort on the Eastern front, the Reich began sending hundreds of thousands of workmen against their will to Germany. In France, the establishment of the compulsory labour organisation *(Service du Travail Obligatoire)* in 1943 by the Vichy government forced large numbers of young 20- to 22-year-olds to join them... or to go underground.

The German system was established everywhere, with a multitude of constraints, from bans on youth groups to the prohibition of carrier pigeons or weapons for hun-

German troops in Sainte-Marie-du-Mont.

Provisions: a perpetual source of anxiety.

ting, including the banning of the use of cameras outside one's own home, and listening to British radio. People could no longer move about freely. The coastal regions were declared out of bounds and every evening the relentless curfew meant that the inhabitants could no longer leave their homes as and when they pleased.

The Occupier responded to the Resistance's first armed initiatives against its troops with the brutal execution of hostages. Then followed massive deportations to the death camps. From France alone, nearly 160,000 men .and women were sent to concentration or extermination camps: members of the Resistance, victims of raids, or simply – for half of them – because they were Jews. This is what the Nazi occupation had meant in all the countries vanquished by the Reich's armies for the previous four years. This is why the perspective of an Allied invasion, synonymous with the return of liberty, inspired such desperate hope. The Normans, perhaps more than

others, knew the full weight of the occupation. It had been particularly oppressive in 1940, by reason of Normandy's proximity to England; it became unbearable in the first months of 1944. The Germans were not blind to the threat of invasion throughout north-western France, from Brittany to the Pas-de-Calais, and hastened to reinforce their defensive system there. The coastal areas were transformed into a massive building site, whose workforce was in large part recruited locally. For several months, the Normans, like the Bretons, the Picards, and the people of the Nord, had literally been reduced to hard labour. New troops, which had to be lodged and fed, poured in unceasingly. The fragile equilibrium of the provisioning system was completely overturned by the influx of extra mouths to be fed. In the towns, the supply of meat, which had hitherto been a mere trickle, dried up completely and disappeared from the butchers' blocks.

The execution of a patriot.

The threat of "the invasion" made the Germans jumpier and more irascible every day. The Gestapo stepped up arrests. The prisons were full. In March, the occupier ordered the confiscation of all the wireless sets in Normandy, with the intention of making it impossible for the population to tune in to Radio London, as it had been doing since 1940 in spite of all the bans. Yes, the German presence had become intolerable, but the dull thuds of the explosions that night of 5th to 6th June were the beginnings of the suggestion that it might be over. The hours passed and the persistent thunder in the distance bolstered the conviction that this time something greater than just another bombing mission was under way. At half past two in the morning, the sirens blared across Caen: the 1,020th air raid warning since the beginning of the Occupation. Maybe the last? The violence of the attack on the coast was such that it could be heard

as far inland as Lisieux, Falaise and Vire. Many a Norman did not sleep that night, torn between the hope of deliverance and the fear of seeing the battle rage through Normandy; henceforth no-one could be in any doubt: this was indeed the invasion.

Indeed, several hours previously General Eisenhower, the Commander-in-Chief of the Allied forces on the Western front, had launched operation Overlord, whose final objective was the liberation of Europe.

From 23h30 on 5th June, the RAF's heavy bombers had gone into action from the Val-de-Saire as far as the east of the Orne. All night, wave upon wave, 1,100 aircraft were to bombard the ten German coastal artillery batteries considered to be the most dangerous, showering them with 6,000 large calibre projectiles. At the dead of this night in June 1944, the vanguard of the Allied armies began to strike.

WITH THE "RED BERETS", BETWEEN THE ORNE AND THE DIVES

The soldiers of freedom came first from the skies. By the first hours of 6th June, airborne troops had already set foot on Norman soil: British to the east, Americans to the west, charged with protecting both flanks of the landing sector and holding back any eventual German counter-attacks. The British paratroopers in General Gale's 6th Airborne Division, the Red Berets, were given the mission of taking control of the zone situated inland from the coast between the Orne estuary and the Dives.

The Channel stopped you, but not us.
Remember Coventry, Plymouth, Bristol, London.
Now it's our turn.

Horsa and Hamilcar gliders, which were towed by Halifax bombers, ready for take off on an airfield in the south of England.

Pegasus Bridge

Shortly before 23h00 on 5th June, six Horsa gliders, towed by bombers, took off from the Tarrant Rushton airfield in Dorset. At 15 minutes past midnight they were uncoupled at 6,000 feet above Cabourg, and descended rapidly towards the earth. Beneath them, the wan glint of two long silver ribbons glimmered in the moonlight: the Orne and its canal. On board were Major John Howard and the men of the "Ox and Bucks" D Company, one of the 6th Airborne's regiments.

They were to capture and preserve the two interconnecting bridges that constituted the sole passage from east to west banks between Caen and the sea. The possession of this strategic position would allow the troops that were to land on the coast some few hours later to come and reinforce the paratroops in a sector where the German reaction was expected to be forceful.

The audacity of the plan was remarkable and Major Howard and his commandos had spent months in training in Britain. But this was no mere exercise. The earth seemed to rise up to meet them at great speed. The Bénouville swing bridge, its metal carcass astride the canal, was right there. In spite of its brake parachute, the leading glider landed making a fearful din, at over 60 mph

in a flurry of sparks resulting from the skids striking the towpath stones. The craft slowed to a halt with its nose in barbed wire, less than fifty yards from its objective. Miraculously, there was no reaction from the enemy guards. Howard and his companions, stunned at first, rapidly got their wits back about them and regrouped for the assault as two other gliders were arriving in their turn. Suddenly, veritable devils with faces smeared black stormed the startled Germans, throwing grenades into their shelters and furiously firing bursts from their machine pistols. In a few minutes, the objective was emptied of opposition, the small garrison wiped out or fleeing. Bénouville Bridge had just entered the history books. It was re-baptised "Pegasus Bridge" after the flying horse insignia worn by the British airborne troops. During the assault, however, the group lost one man: Lieutenant Brotheridge, the first Allied soldier to die in combat on Norman soil on this 6th June 1944.

Not far from there, the men who had flown in on two of the second group's gliders (the third got lost) captured the swing bridge over the Orne at Ranville, without encountering any resistance. Mission accomplished. The radio operator frenetically transmitted the code indicating their success: "Ham and Jam... Ham and Jam..."

The capture of the Merville battery

This first action had barely been brought to its successful conclusion before the bulk of the 6ᵗʰ Airborne was dropping into the zone between the Orne and the Dives. Hundreds of parachutes opened and descended earthwards in a sky glaringly lit by the beams of the enemy's projectors and tracer fire, but the wind, fire from the FLAK (anti-aircraft defence) and the mediocre beaconing on the ground put in place by the scouts resulted in a wide-ranging dispersion of the troops. Some men fell in the flooded marshes along the Dives, others in the Bavent woods. Many were to wander for hours before finding their units, attempting to follow the sound of hunting horns and whistles. The uprooting of the "Rommel's asparagus" cluttering the fields was delayed, whereas gliders bringing reinforcements and heavy equipment were soon to arrive. Above all, this confusion was a threat to the accomplishment of the series of specific missions entrusted to certain units; they were achieved, however, thanks mainly to the heroics of a few handfuls of "Red Berets". Lieutenant-Colonel Otway was to capture the Merville battery, whose four 150-mm guns posed a threat to the landing beaches close to the Orne estuary. Otway only managed to assemble 150 or so of his men for the assault on this veritable stronghold, surrounded by barbed wire, minefields, and defended by nearly 200 German soldiers. Six hundred men were missing. Worse, the aerial bombardment had completely missed its target and the system of defences was still intact. As for the gliders that were to have landed directly on the target, none hit the mark. All their carefully laid plans, so often rehearsed in Great Britain, were laid waste. They would have to improvise. At 04h30, they launched the assault. Having broken through the barbed wire using Bangalore torpedoes, the paratroops burst into the area surrounding the battery and captured it after a quarter of an hour of vicious hand-to-hand fighting, which cost the lives of nearly all the defenders and put half of the assailants out of action. An unpleasant surprise awaited them: the dreaded weapons turned out to be only 100-mm guns, practically inoffensive for the landing beaches.

The troops of the 6ᵗʰ Airborne blackening their faces before the assault, so as to be less visible at night.

Major Howard's three gliders landed right next to Bénouville Bridge.

An audacious coup in Troarn

Meanwhile, Major Roseveare had become lost in the Norman countryside with a few dozen men. He landed over 6 miles from his objective, the village of Troarn, site of the largest of the five bridges over the Dives, which had to be destroyed rapidly to prevent German reinforcements from crossing the river. Although they managed to recuperate trailers and explosives, there was no sign of the jeeps that were also supposed to have come in by glider. So the little troop set out on foot, pushing and hauling their dead-weight burdens. After several hours of struggle and slow-going, they came across a jeep full of medicine. The providential vehicle was immediately requisitioned and unloaded. Major Rosevaere and half a dozen of his men attached one of the trailers, got on board and made straight for Troarn, whereas the rest of

"Pegasus Bridge" after it had been captured.

Ranville: many gliders landed with difficulty, crashing into walls and houses.

A jeep and its trailer being off-loaded from a "Horsa" glider.

the troop was sent to the bridges at Bures. Shortly after 5 o'clock in the morning, the commando unit stormed the village, machine-gunning down a German, which brought the whole garrison into the street. Under a hail of bullets, Major Rosevaere drove the gauntlet of the village with his foot to the floor, miraculously escaping being hit, but losing one of his men in the process, who

had been hit or had fallen during the mad charge. Down below lay the river. As the bridge was not guarded, a few minutes were all it took to lay the charges on one of the arches; the bridge blew at 5h20, along with the trailer filled with explosives left on it. In the course of the next few hours, the bridges at Bures and Robehomme met the same fate.

Many isolated paratroopers were captured by the Germans.

On board a Stirling bomber, converted into a troop carrier, paratroops joking to bolster their courage before the plunge into the unknown.

WITH THE SKY TROOPS

FROM THE DAILY TELEGRAPH CORRESPONDENT
LEONARD MOSLEY

AT TWO MINUTES PAST ONE THIS MORNING I PARACHUTED INTO EUROPE – SIX-AND-A-HALF HOURS BEFORE OUR SEABORNE FORCES BEGAN THE FULL SCALE INVASION.

IT WAS FIVE MINUTES TO ONE WHEN THE LIGHT SNAPPED OFF AND A DOOR IN THE PLANE WAS OPENED. UNDER IT WE COULD SEE THE COAST OF FRANCE. FLAK FROM THE COAST DEFENCES WAS SPOUTING FLAME EVERYWHERE.

THE RED LIGHT FLASHED AND SWIFTLY CHANGED TO GREEN, AND WE WERE ALL SHUFFLING DOWN THE HOLD AND JUMPING INTO SPACE. WE KNEW THAT WE WERE GOING DOWN INTO ENEMY TERRITORY COVERED WITH POLES AND HOLES, AND THICK WITH NAZIS WAITING FOR US. I LOOKED, AS I TWISTED DOWN, FOR THE CHURCH I HAD BEEN TOLD TO USE AS A LANDMARK, BUT THE WIND CAUGHT ME AND WAS WHISKING ME EAST. I CAME DOWN IN AN ORCHARD OUTSIDE A FARMHOUSE.

AS I STOOD UP WITH MY HARNESS OFF AND WIPED THE SWEAT OFF MY BROWN-PAINTED FACE, I KNEW I WAS HOPELESSLY LOST. DARE I GO TO THE FARMHOUSE AND ASK FOR DIRECTIONS? SUDDENLY THERE WAS A RIP AND TEAR IN MY FLAPPING JUMPING-SMOCK, AND I FLUNG MYSELF TO THE GROUND AS MACHINE GUNS RATTLED. THERE WERE TWO SMA-SHING EXPLOSIONS – HAND GRENADES. I COULD NOW SEE FIGURES MANOEUVRING IN THE MOONLIGHT. I DIVED THROUGH A TANGLE OF BARBED WIRE INTO THE NEXT FIELD, AND BEGAN TO RUN AT THE CROUCH.

THEN, SUDDENLY, AT THE FARTHER EDGE, THERE WERE TWO MORE FIGURES, AND THEY WERE COMING TOWARDS ME, CARRYING GUNS. THERE WAS A CRASH OF STEN-GUN FIRE, AND BOTH MEN CRUMPLED UP NOT FIFTEEN YARDS FROM ME. INTO THE FIELD STEALTHILY CAME FIVE MEN TO CHALLENGE ME – AND I WAS WITH OUR OWN PARATROOPS AGAIN.

FOR TWO LONG, WEARY HOURS WE WANDERED THE COUNTRY. WE HID FROM GERMAN PATROLS IN FRENCH BARNS. WE SHOT UP A NAZI CAR SPEEDING DOWN A LANE. A YOUTH APPEARED WITH A GERMAN FLASK FULL OF FRENCH WINE, AND AFTER WE HAD DRUNK IT, HE LED US AWAY FROM THE ENEMY. JUST AFTER 3 A. M. WE MADE OUR RENDEZVOUS.

AMERICAN PARATROOPS JUMP OVER THE COTENTIN

Where the British troops' parachute drop was far from perfect, the Americans' was downright messy. Around 1 o'clock in the morning, 432 C-47 *Dakotas* carrying 6,600 paratroops belonging to General Maxwell Taylor's 101st US Airborne Division were flying into the coast of the Cotentin from the west. On board, nervous men joked to keep their spirits up, some going over their instructions for the nth time, others chewing gum with a fixed stare. They would certainly have been much more worried had they been aware of Air Chief Marshal Leigh-Mallory's predictions of losses higher than 50%. A gravely worried Eisenhower had hesitated for a long time before giving the go-ahead to the operation. He finally came around to it, given the absolute necessity of taking possession of the hinterland and the access roads to the beaches of the eastern Cotentin. Without this protection, the American division that was to land there, down the beach from the Varreville dunes, would likely be repelled into the sea.

A moment nervous tension, a few seconds before taking the plunge.

General Eisenhower, Commander-in-Chief of operation Overlord, talking with the men of the 101ˢᵗ Airborne.

A deadly game of hide and seek in the Normandy night

01h15. The planes arrived over the drop zone. The anti-aircraft *FLAK* barrage intensified. A plane took a direct hit, burst into flames and smashed into the ground in a gigantic fireball. Most of the C-47 pilots were neophytes. This was a terrifying baptism by fire for them. They attempted to get out of danger by climbing steeply, by accelerating or by swerving and vee-

ring, resulting in catastrophic drops. The paratroops were dispersed over an area 25 miles by 15. Some even fell straight into the sea.

Scarcely one thousand men managed to regroup quickly to accomplish their mission, and particularly to capture the battery at Saint-Martin-de-Varreville. For the rest, lost and disorientated in the Cotentin's maze

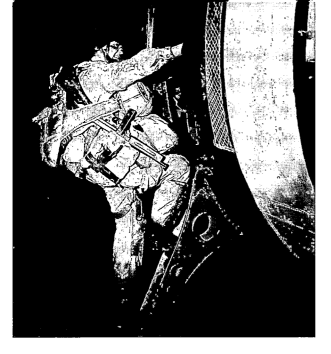

Heavily loaded paratroops boarding the C-47 Dakotas.

Sainte-Mère-Eglise: paratroops trying to dislodge an isolated sniper.

of tiny hedged fields, where every hedge could hide friend or foe alike, began a long night of anguish, senses straining. General Taylor himself was isolated for several long minutes, and embraced the first soldier he met out of sheer joy. All night long, shots rang out wherever chance flung the small groups of paratroops and the Germans who had set out to hunt them down together. A deadly game of hide and seek under the debonair gaze of the Norman cattle ruminating uninterruptedly in perfect serenity.

The 82ⁿᵈ and 101ˢᵗ Airborne sustained heavy losses.

The 82ⁿᵈ Airborne's capture of Sainte-Mère-Eglise

Shortly before two o'clock in the morning, it was the turn of the men of the 82ⁿᵈ Airborne, under the command of General Ridgeway, to jump over French soil. The division was initially to have gone into action around Saint-Sauveur-le-Vicomte, in order to prepare the cordoning off of the Cotentin peninsula. But Rommel, who was aware of the vital importance of the zone with regard to the defence of Cherbourg, had foresightedly stationed extra troops at this exact spot. Allied high command had modified its plans at the last minute in order to avoid a predictable slaughter, having been alerted to the situation by the Resistance. The 82ⁿᵈ would go into action further east and support the 101ˢᵗ on either side of the Merderet. They didn't know that the Germans had flooded the marshlands much more extensively than the aerial photographs taken over the preceding weeks sugges-

ted. Terrible snares of mud and water hidden under thick grass awaited the paratroops. Tangled in their harnesses and laden with equipment weighing between 30 and 40 kilos, some drowned right there, without glory, before even having fought. Air Chief Marshal Leigh-Mallory's sinister predictions were close to becoming reality. Fortunately, one of the division's three regiments, the 505ᵗʰ, escaped disaster and succeeded in landing near its objective, the village of Sainte-Mère-Eglise. Too near, in the case of some groups, which landed smack in the middle of the village, where the members of the German garrison, who were there because a house had accidentally caught fire, hewed them down with machine guns under the alarmed stare of the inhabitants and their mayor, Alexandre Renaud. However, the enemy finally packed their bags and headed for Carentan, alarmed by the

Paratroopers meeting the first Normans to be liberated.

hundreds of planes that were emerging from the clouds, flying low with all their lights on, and by the multitude of parachutes that were descending around them. At 04h30, a battalion led by Lieutenant-Colonel Edward Krause captured Sainte-Mère-Eglise, without fighting. As a sign of victory, the Americans, who were firmly decided to defend their first success, hung their flag on the door of the town hall.

Many gliders crash-landed.
General Don Pratt, Lieutenant-Commander of the 101ˢᵗ Airborne, met his death this way.

"THE DICE ARE CAST"

While many Normans were wondering what the noises of battle might mean, a handful of them knew just what was going on. During the evening of 5th June, over the **BBC** airwaves, the leaders of the Resistance heard the messages they had waited for for so long: the signal that the invasion had started. *"Les dés sont sur le tapis"* (*"The dice are cast"*), was the order to launch *"plan Vert"*, the sabotage of railway lines. *"Il fait chaud à Suez"* (*"It's hot in Suez"*), was the code for *"plan Tortue"* aiming at the paralysis of the road network, to prevent reinforcements from reaching to the coast. *"Plan Violet"* consisted in destroying the telephone lines... Everywhere, small groups of the **FFI** *(Forces Françaises de l'Intérieur)* Resistance fighters went into action. Trees lining the roads were felled using explosives, or with saws if none were available. Signposts were torn up or turned back to front. The roads were strewn with hundreds of tyre-puncturing devices and mines. Telegraph poles were destroyed and lines cut. In spite of the guards, several railway lines were put out of service using dynamite or by unbolting the rails.

No-one dared to wake the Führer, stuffed with sleeping pills, during the night of 5th-6th June.

The Resistance, alerted by messages from the BBC, preparing their weapons.

All this merely increased the very singular disorder reigning in the German camp that decisive night. The intelligence services of the 15th Army, stationed in Picardy and in the Pas-de-Calais, had managed to identify the meaning of one of the personal messages. Although it was not destined for the whole Resistance, as they thought, but to a specific network, the consequences were the same. As they waited for Verlaine's famous lines "...bercent mon coeur d'une langueur monotone" (...soothe my heart with monotonous languor), broadcast 48 hours after: "Les sanglots longs des violons d'automne..." (The soughing sobs of autumn's violins...), the Germans knew, on 5th June, that the invasion was imminent. Warned of this, General von Salmuth placed his 15th Army on general alert. He then immediately informed the headquarters of the "B" Group of Armies in La Roche Guyon, whence Rommel had departed the day before to go to Germany. The Commander in Chief in the West, Marshal von Rundstedt, in Saint-Germain-en-Laye

was also notified. Nevertheless, following an incredible lapse into negligence, this vital piece of intelligence was not transmitted to the 7th Army, the very one defending the whole sector between the Loire and the Dives, where the decisive events were about to happen. So its commanding officer, General Dollman, did nothing to modify his plans: he summoned all the division commanders in his sector to Le Mans for the morning of 6th June, for a battle simulation-type war game. Those who were coming from furthest away were already en route.

The "plan Vert" organised the systematic sabotage of the railways, to hamper the arrival of German reinforcements in Normandy.

Marshal Rommel, lulled into a false sense of security by the bad weather in the Channel, left for Germany on the morning of 5th June.

In Saint-Lô, one of his subordinates, General Marcks, Commander of the 84th Army Corps in charge of the Manche and Calvados coastline, was peacefully celebrating his 53rd birthday with his closest colleagues. He was only made aware of the first Allied airdrops in his sector at 01h30 in the small hours of morning. Even then, the information was patchy and contradictory. Some of the paratroops indicated in these reports were mere dummies, carrying fireworks that imitated the sound of weapons fire. At 02h10 the *Kriegsmarine* telephoned Rommel's staff HQ: "*We can hear engines off the eastern Cotentin. All our radar stations are out of action. We have no more detailed information than that.*" The general staff replied half an hour later: "*Here, we do not think that this is an operation on any substantial scale.*" To make matters worse, communications were breaking down: the Resistance had cut the German army's heavy-duty underground cables linking Cherbourg, Saint-Lô, Rennes, Le Mans and Paris in several places. Indecisiveness and procrastination reigned in the upper echelons of the *Wehrmacht*. Was this really the main invasion, or a simple manoeuvre, a diversionary tactic designed to draw attention away from the principal attack which could be happening elsewhere? The German chiefs of staff had been expecting an Allied offensive in the Pas-de-Calais. The *Kriegsmarine* and the *Luftwaffe* were of this opinion, and even von Rundstedt had come close to agreeing with them. In Berlin, General Jodl, who didn't dare have the Führer woken, advocated prudence and refused to authorise the armoured divisions held in reserve to mobilise and head for Normandy.

Plunged into the greatest perplexity, the German high command's reaction during these critical few hours was slow and indecisive. It did not believe in the reality of a major operation. It was wrong. The great invasion had begun. Dawn was soon to rise on D-Day, the culmination of the lengthy and colossal preparatory exercise that had been worked on over the preceding years on the other side of the Channel, whose aim was the scaling and destruction of the famous Atlantic Wall, and the liberation of Europe from the shackles of the Nazi regime.

The bombardments and the sabotage organised by the Resistance profoundly disorganised German communications.

The Allied bombardments of the radar stations in the Manche and the North Sea blinded the German remote sensing system. In the picture, radar station FuMo 214 in Arromanches, destroyed a few days before the Landings.

THE FOUR-YEAR WAIT

"We have fortified the coast of Europe from Northern Norway to Mediterranean, and it is armed with the most implacable weapons the 20th Century has to offer.
This is why an enemy attack, however powerful and furious it may be, is doomed to failure.
At Dieppe, they only lasted nine hours, and that was before the Wall was built. If they last nine hours next time, they will be doing well!"

Joseph Goëbbels,
Propaganda Minister of the Third Reich.

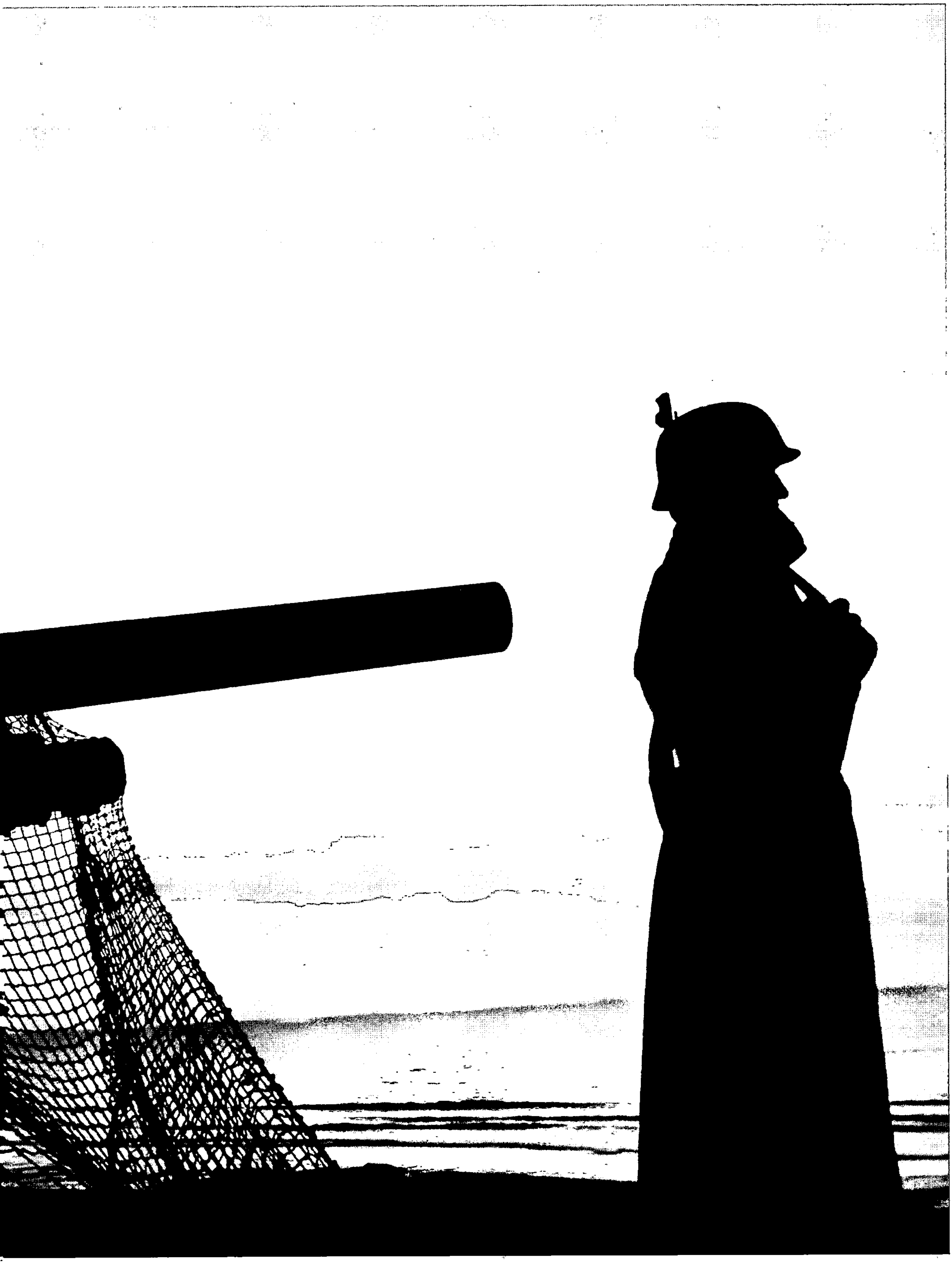

THE ATLANTIC WALL

The construction of the Atlantic Wall was ordered by Hitler in December 1941. This decision was a logical development in the general evolution of the war in Europe. Over the preceding six months, Hitler's armies had invaded the USSR, but had not succeeded in defeating the Red Army as quickly as had been anticipated. It had become obvious that the campaign was to be a long one and it became necessary to re-deploy contingents from the troops stationed in the West in ever increasing numbers. In order to compensate for this weakening of the defences there, and faced with the threat of a possible enemy initiative, reinforced by the United States' entry into the war, Hitler resolved to edify an impenetrable rampart all along the coasts of western Europe, which he intended to transform into an impregnable fortress. Nazi propagandists were quick to baptise it "Atlantikwall".

Fortress Europe

The Todt Organisation was given responsibility for the immense task of erecting defences along the 3,000 miles and more of coastline from the Netherlands to the Spanish border, then along the Mediterranean coast after the invasion of the unoccupied zone at the end of 1942. It consisted of 450,000 volunteers and forced labourers (of whom 300,000 worked solely in France), locals and foreigners (Czechs, Italians, Poles, North-Africans...) placed under the orders of German supervisors. No less than eleven million tonnes of concrete and one million tonnes of reinforcing steel rods were needed to build the 15,000 structures of differing sizes, of which some had walls over 2 metres thick.

Far from being a veritable "wall" like the Great Wall of China, the *Atlantikwall* was a discontinuous aggregation of separate defensive systems of unequal density and designed for purposes that differed from region to region.

Eleven million tonnes of concrete and one million tonnes of reinforcing steel rods were needed to build the 15,000 fortifications strung out along the Atlantic coasts.

Hundreds of thousands of men, volunteers and forced labourers, participated in the construction of the Atlantic Wall.

A building under construction.

Roughly speaking there were three main types of fortification: the fortresses, the coastal artillery batteries, and the operational bases and resistance points. Early on, the German high command latched on to the idea that the Allies, with their highly mechanised army, would inevitably try to capture a port, in order to be able to land their essential assault equipment more easily and, later, the provisions and supplies necessary for the combat troops. The attack on Dieppe in 1942 only served to reinforce this belief. Consequently, the main ports on the North Sea and the Channel were transformed into fortresses *(Festungen)*. These bristled with weapons, large-bore and long-range artillery, which would serve as protection against a landing fleet and prevent one from approaching the shore. The Seine Bay was thus protected by two fortresses, one in Cherbourg and the other in Le Havre.

Coastal artillery batteries manned by the army or the navy were established between these fortresses. Separated by a few kilometres, they were as a general rule equipped with between four and six medium-bore guns, set into trenches or in pillboxes. As with the fortresses, their main mission was firing out to sea, on an eventual invasion fleet. On the coast of Lower Normandy between Le Havre and Cherbourg, there were thirty-odd coastal artillery batteries (more often than not equipped with guns with a calibre ranging from 100-mm to 155-mm).

The Todt Organisation workers were supervised by Germans.

General von Salmuth, Commander of the 15ᵗʰ Army, inspecting installations.

Checking out the German propaganda.

The resistance points (*Widerstandnesten*, designated in German military terminology by the acronym WN) were, generally, smaller installations, occupying areas of a few hundred square yards and designed to be local shore-based defences against assault troops. They consisted of one or two bunkers, equipped with medium-bore guns, generally laid out to cover a beach with cross-fire; *Tobruks*, (concrete vats buried in the ground with a circular opening at the top for a machine-gunner), anti-aircraft guns, mortar and machine-gun positions, all linked by a network of trenches and surrounded by barbed wire. There were fifteen or so *Widerstandnesten* along the 3₁/₂ miles of beach between Vierville and Colleville (the future Omaha beach). A concentration of resistance points could constitute an operational base *(Stützpunkt).* The one governing the Seulles estuary consisted

of three. These defences, much more so than the coastal batteries, were to prove devastatingly efficient on the morning of 6ᵗʰ June.

The construction of the Atlantic Wall began for real in the spring of 1942 and accelerated noticeably during 1943, but this titanic task was far from complete at the beginning of 1944 when Marshal Rommel arrived in France.

A bunker camouflaged to look like a house.

The Wall: myth or reality?

Pictures of the Atlantic Wall in newspapers, on postcards, posters and the cinema newsreels conjured up a singularly one-sided impression. They invariably showed the formidable bastions in the Pas-de-Calais: the Lindeman battery and its gigantic 406-mm cannons, the Todt battery and its 380-mm guns... but the reality was less reassuring in many other places, where the fortifications were neither as dense nor as powerful. Marshal Gerd von Rundstedt, Commander-in-Chief of the Western front, was not seduced by the alluring sirens of Nazi propaganda. He gave little credence to the invulnerability of the Atlantic Wall and did

not refrain from saying so: *"The Wall was a myth. Nothing in front of it; nothing behind it. Just a piece of decoration! You had to see it to understand what it really was. It had no depth and did not extend far. It was a simple piece of bluff, more aimed at fooling the German people than the enemy. In the most optimistic of scenarios, it could have held up an invading enemy for 24 hours. A violent assault, lasting a day, led by a resolute force, would be sufficient to break through the line at any given point... I told the Führer this in October 1943, but he didn't want to hear it."*

In November 1943 Marshal Rommel, the famous "Desert Fox", who had been repatriated to Germany from North

The Widerstandnesten, equipped with medium-bore guns, were designed for the short range defence of the beaches.

Marshal Rommel and his general staff inspecting the beach defences.

A Belgian gate, a defensive obstacle salvaged from the Maginot Line.

Africa nine months previously, was charged by Hitler with the mission of inspecting the Atlantic Wall. Almost immediately afterwards, he was appointed to the command of Army Group "B", in charge of the coastal sector stretching from the Netherlands to the Loire estuary, the very sector in which the Anglo-American invasion attempt would most probably take place. Contrary to his superior, Marshal von Rundstedt, he believed that the Atlantic Wall could play a role in countering an attack by the Allies, who he considered it would be necessary to contain on the beaches. Thus, during the first five months of 1944, he deployed an abundance of energy in reinforcing it, particularly on the Seine Bay coast, where he had noted many deficiencies. These deficiencies were all the more serious as, to his way of thinking – and contrary to the ideas held by the majority of the German top brass, who were convinced that the invasion would come in the Pas-de-Calais – this sector seemed particularly exposed to the threat of an invasion. Rommel gave the construction of the Atlantic Wall its second wind.

Concrete pillboxes were swiftly thrown together in order to provide protection from attacks from the air for the coastal artillery that still lacked it. Detailed attention was given to the short-range defence systems covering the beaches. To this end, Rommel multiplied the *Widerstandnesten*. On his orders, the shores were covered with all sorts of obstacles: "Czech hedgehogs", "nut-crackers", "Belgian gates" etc.; the Allies' landing barges were to crash into, become impaled upon, be gutted and blown up by these diabolical traps. The access roads to the beaches were blocked by anti-tank walls or "dragons' teeth", the dunes were transformed into a tangled mess of barbed wire, studded with machine gun trenches and flame-throwers. Inland, and applying a method he had effectively employed in Libya, he caused hundreds of thousands of mines to be laid. In order to counter assaults by airborne troops, the low-lying land was voluntarily flooded and large, menacing stakes, the famous "*Rommel's Asparagus*", pointed at the sky in the open spaces where gliders might have landed.

Behind the Wall: the Wehrmacht

The value of a defensive system such as the Atlantic Wall was not merely reliant on the fortifications it was composed of, nor the number and position of the guns housed within them, but also – and perhaps primarily – on the troops stationed behind or close to it, their number, their competence, and the strategic or tactical use the high command intended to make of them. What was the nature of the *Wehrmacht's* troops on the Western front in spring 1944?

In 1942, von Rundstedt could only count on between 25 and 30 divisions for the defence of Western Europe as the Eastern front was absorbing a major proportion of the available units. At the end of 1943, Hitler decided to reinforce the units on the Western front considerably, as he sensed that the threat of an Anglo-American invasion was coming closer. In the middle of the month of June 1944, there were 58 divisions there, that is to say about 700,000 men. Von Rundstedt used these reinforcements to fill out the lines along the North Sea and the Channel, giving priority to the Pas-de-Calais, the sector where General von Salmuth's 15th Army was stationed and, to a lesser

A *"nut-cracker"*: the landing barges would trigger the explosion of the attached mines when they ran over the metal beams.

extent, the Seine Bay area, under the responsibility of General Dollman's 7th Army.

The quality of the troops was rather uneven. Alongside at least fifteen well trained and well equipped infantry divisions, or the storm-paratroops in Brittany, there were also thirty-odd so-called "static" coastal defence divisions, not having rapid or mechanised transport facilities.

A beach covered with "Czech hedgehogs".

The 21ˢᵗ Panzer was the only German armoured division to be stationed near the coast of Normandy, around Saint-Pierre-sur-Dives.

Their artillery, which was somewhat miscellaneous, was horse-drawn and the only means of transportation available to the troops was in many cases the bicycle. Their average age, often advanced, did not conjure up visions of heroic feats in battle, no more so than did the Eastern volunteers' units, the "*Osttruppen*", or in other words former Soviet prisoners of war who had been integrated into the German Army with or without their consent. The phrase attributed to General von Schlieben, Commander of the 709ᵗʰ Infantry Division, stationed in the North of the Cotentin, is now famous: "*It seems unlikely that we will be able to make Russians fight for Germany in France against Americans...*"

In fact, the trump cards in the German army pack were the 10 armoured divisions of the *Panzergruppen West*, commanded by General Geyr von Schweppenburg, with

their 170,000 men and their 1,500 tanks: a task force that was as impressive as it was formidable. Their deployment was the object of a serious controversy within the most elevated spheres of the *Wehrmacht*. Schweppenburg, with support from von Rundstedt, intended keeping them in reserve, a good way back from the coasts, in order to have the capability to organise a massive armoured counter-offensive to wipe out their adversaries after having allowed them to land. Rommel, on the other hand, wanted to spread them out along the coast in order to repel the invaders back into the sea, without waiting and allowing them to receive reinforcements. Hitler proposed a compromise solution... by splitting the forces, which gave no-one satisfaction, all the more so as any movement of the armoured divisions required direct and personal authorisation from the Führer himself anyway. On several occasions Rommel requested permission to bring the

Panzer Lehr and the 12th *SS Hitlerjugend* to each side of the Vire estuary, where he feared an Anglo-American attack might come (not without reason), but in vain.

We cannot imagine what would have happened had he been given satisfaction.

Whereas the land-based forces (the *Heer*), in spite of a certain lack of homogeneity between its units, generally offered sound guarantees of solidity, this could not have been said of the *Kriegsmarine* and the *Luftwaffe*, both of which were severely depleted at the time the Allies were on the verge of launching the decisive assault.

The period when the *Luftwaffe* had terrorised its adversaries was ended. It was now reduced to a defensive role, and with drastically reduced means. Marshal Sperrle, Commander of the 3rd *Luftflotte*, had 300,000 ground staff some of whom, because they were surplus, were deployed in the Luftwaffe's mediocre campaign divisions, but this overstaffing only concerned the ground crews: he lacked the core essentials – planes, and pilots to fly them. Since the end of 1943, the Anglo-American air raids on Germany had resulted in the melting away of reserves like snow in sunshine. In the spring of 1944, Sperrle had a mere thousand planes... only half of which were fit to fly. He was forced to watch impotently as his aerodromes, in a large circle around the future landing sector, were methodically destroyed by Allied bombing raids. What could he have done with his feeble contingent on the decisive day, when faced with Eisenhower's 11,000 aircraft?

The situation of the naval forces in the West was barely any better. Between the North Sea and the Atlantic, Admiral Krancke only had 50 warships, none of which was bigger than a destroyer, and a miscellaneous flotilla of a few hundred patrol boats and minelayers at his disposal, with which to respond to the thousands of boats of the massed Allied armada waiting in the English ports. His principal strike force was made up of thirty-odd torpedo boats and fast motor launches based in Boulogne, Le

A "Teller" mine atop a stake.

Havre and Cherbourg. As for the submarines, their utilisation remained stringently hypothetical, as they were still under the direct control of Admiral Doenitz and Hitler himself.

When it came to their enemy's offensive, therefore, the *Wehrmacht* was mainly to count on the Atlantic Wall's effectiveness, and on the troops amassed behind it. As for the Allies, they were perfectly aware of the risks involved and did not for one minute under-estimate the strength of the opposition awaiting them. Having given long consideration to the strategy finally to be chosen for the re-conquest of Europe, they had begun actively and meticulously preparing the landings on the Normandy beaches as early as 1943, so as to have all the trump cards in hand.

"Volunteers" from Turkestan, recruited into the German army, in the area around Deauville.

THE ALLIES' PREPARATIONS FOR D-DAY

The idea of an invasion of the French coasts was not new. It had formed in Winston Churchill's mind during the darkest days. *"We'll be back,"* as he had said defiantly in June 1940, as His Majesty's Expeditionary Force was being evacuated from Dunkirk and being brought over the Channel in the dramatic circumstances that are now so famous.

"We'll be back" (Winston Churchill, June 1940)

Hitler could hold forth that *"England has been hounded from the continent!"* but on 23rd June 1940, by way of a reply, a British commando unit undertook an audacious strike near Boulogne! This was no mere show of bravado. From this moment on, a Combined Operations General Staff was set up, at first under the command of Admiral Keyes and soon afterwards commanded by Lord Louis Mountbatten, the cousin of the Royal Family.

The Overlord General Staff.
In the foreground, from left to right, : Air Chief Marshal Tedder, General Eisenhower, (Supreme Commander of Allied Forces), General Montgomery. Standing, from left to right, General Bradley, Admiral Ramsay, Air Chief Marshal Leigh-Mallory, General Bedell-Smith.

Terrible losses were sustained by the Allies during the raid on Dieppe in August 1942, but they learned a tremendous amount.

The navy, the air force and the army were ordered to consider jointly the problems that a future invasion of Europe might pose and, in the meantime, to organise a series of coastal raids with the aim of testing the German defences and developing tactics and equipment. The British attacked the Lofoten islands and Vaagsö in Norway, the Channel Islands, Spitzberg, then later Bruneval in the Pays de Caux, Saint-Nazaire, Dieppe and elsewhere, demonstrating their unflagging determination, following the lead of their Prime Minister. For long months, however, a major part of their energies was absorbed in the combat they had to win, alone against the Axis: they had to defend and preserve their own territory, which was under the threat of invasion, and there was also the struggle in the Mediterranean, on the Atlantic, in Greece, and in the Libyan desert...

The year 1941 was the first major turning point in the Second World War. The attack on the USSR, launched in June, swallowed up an increasing number of German divisions in the East, obliging Hitler to adopt a defensive strategy in the West from that moment on. The Atlantic Wall would not be long in appearing. In December, the Japanese attack on Pearl Harbour pitched the American giant into the conflict. A few days later Roosevelt and Churchill met in Washington and sketched out a common strategy. Germany was identified as the enemy to be crushed as a priority. To this purpose, the Americans began sending men, weapons and ammunition to the British Isles, or at least in as much as was possible, because, for the time being, submarines were still the masters of the Atlantic and crossing it was a particularly perilous proposition.

This choice was not endorsed by all the American high command and, more importantly, it did not unite public opinion, which was more interested in seeing a major initiative undertaken against the Japanese in the Pacific. It was in consequence necessary to demonstrate that the *"Germany first"* strategy was the right one.

Checking parachutes in an American factory.

From "Round up" to "Overlord"

For this reason, the Americans, who suspected nothing, were in a hurry to join the fray. From the month of April 1942, the head of general staff, General George Marshal, arrived in London with several possible plans for the invasion of France in his briefcase. The main one was code-named "Round up". It provided for a landing somewhere between Boulogne and Le Havre deploying fifty divisions or so with support from 6,000 aircraft and 7,000 ships. Churchill warmly approved of the project's concept... albeit demonstrating more than customary reserve with regard to its chances of success in the near future. No-one could have guessed that they were to wait another 26 months before it was pulled off.

In fact, two divergent conceptions were not slow to surface in the Allied camp. For the American officers, trained at West Point in theory inspired by that practised by Napoleon, they had to strike *"du fort au fort"*, meaning attacking Germany by the shortest possible route leading to the heart of the Reich; or in other words, invade immediately on the Channel or North Sea coast and smash a way through into the Ruhr valley. The British were not very enthusiastic about this idea, which they judged to be premature. "Fortress Europe" appeared to them to be a formidable proposition, especially at that particular point. Had not the tragic episode in Dieppe in 1942 taught them that lesson? A hastily prepared enterprise ran the risk of ending in disaster. So they recommended another method, precisely that which had been used to good effect against Napoleon in days gone by, the "bullfight strategy": you first weaken and leave your opponents out of breath by sticking *banderillas* into him in a series of peripheral attacks ... before delivering the fatal blow.

As the Allies were still a long way from being able to gather together the forces necessary for the accomplishment of "Round up", Churchill convinced the others that the operation could not be envisaged until the spring of 1943. In the short term, he suggested an attack against French North Africa, as they could anticipate only feeble resistance from the Vichy government's troops stationed there. Roosevelt and his generals came round to this proposition – without excessive enthusiasm – which resulted in operation "Torch", the first of the great Allied landings. After this success, the debate raged again between the Americans and the British. It was to last for several months and often involved bitter wrangling and stormy work sessions. All the more so as Churchill seemed ever more motivated by a new preoccupation: what was to become of the geopolitical configuration of Europe once the Nazis had been eliminated? The progress of the Soviet "allies" since their success in Stalingrad worried him. It was necessary for the Westerners to move faster than the Red Army by penetrating into the centre of the continent as rapidly as possible, through the Balkans ... or Italy!

At the conference in Casablanca in January 1943, Churchill suggested exploiting the favourable situation in the Mediterranean, by landing in Sicily, which would mean a new postponement of "Round up". The American President accepted, but in exchange, obtained the creation of a general staff (COSSAC) specially charged with planning the attack on the north-western coast of France, which he did not intend to renounce. Sicily was captured in July

The factories worked round the clock to supply the Allies with weapons.

(operation "Husky"), leaving the invasion of Italy a single tempting step away. The step was taken in September 1943 (operations "Avalanche" and "Slapstick"). Roosevelt and the American military chiefs allowed themselves to be swayed once more. At least they could console themselves with the idea that this series of landings had allowed the Allies to burnish their weapons and perfect techniques of amphibious assault. Above all, they succeeded, this time, in exchange for this series of concessions, in having their partners agree to formal arrangements concerning the French invasion operation. The "Trident" conference held in Washington in may 1943, fixed the date of the operation, 1st May 1944, and gave it a new code-name: "Overlord".

Thousands of assault barges were needed for the landings.

The Landings to take place in Normandy

There was one year left to bring this project, whose multiple difficulties were to be resolved thanks to gems of imagination, ingenuity... and cunning, to a successful conclusion. In March 1943, General Frederick Morgan took up his duties as Chief of Staff to the Allied Supreme Commander (COSSAC). As he waited for the Supreme Commander to be appointed, it was down to him to start planning the invasion on the other side of the Channel. "This bloody business won't work! But you have to get down to it all the same," as General Brooks, the Commander-in-Chief of the British Army said to him as he was explaining his mission to him. In spite of these discouraging words, Morgan did get down to it, and brought selflessness and clear-sighted perceptiveness to the task. Where should they land? Of all the places considered, from Norway to Portugal, two finished by overshadowing the others: the Pas-de-Calais and the Seine Bay. There were powerful arguments in favour of the first option: it was not far from the English coast, the air cover would be better, the rotation of ships would be faster, allowing enhanced logistical performance, and finally they would be closer to the Reich's borders.

Training on the British coast.

Men of the British 50ᵗʰ Infantry Division examining a scale model of their future assault sector.

It was the choice suggested by reason! The Germans had already made the same choice in their attempts to second-guess their adversaries' intentions. Consequently, the Atlantic Wall was much more robust here than elsewhere, with massive coastal artillery batteries and the best troops – General von Salmuth's 15ᵗʰ Army – massed behind it. The British were thus to opt ... for the Seine Bay, acting in this instance as they did as a general rule, that is to say using their imagination to wrong-foot the Germans by doing the opposite of what their purely military logic could suggest.

The Allies' secret boots

Rommel expected the invasion to come at high tide. As a result, he had placed obstacles to landing barges on the beaches with this in mind. In order to both avoid the traps that had been laid for them and the over-long distance their troops would have to cover at low tide, the Allies were thus to attack at mid-tide, as it was rising. Hitler himself, backed up by his Generals, had decreed that the Anglo-Americans would be bound to attempt to capture a sizeable port, which they would need for re-provisioning purposes. Cherbourg and Le Havre had thus been transformed

into veritable fortresses, as had other sites that were judged to be under threat. The invasion was to take place... between the two, along a shoreline where there were only a few small fishing ports. To succeed in this bold endeavour, the Allies were to have to perfect one of the most stupefying innovations of the war: the artificial harbours, carefully concealed under their code-name "Mulberries". These were another of the inventions inspired by Churchill. He had already played with this singular idea during the Great War; it saw the light of day a quarter of a century later. All the component elements were prefabricated in England and then transported to the Normandy coast, right behind the invasion fleet, then assembled on site. This titanic feat of civil engineering required the creation of many new ship-yards and 40,000 people were mobilised for the purposes of the construction process.

The supplying of fuel to an army as mechanised as that which was to embark on the assault on Europe posed another tricky problem. The solution was to bear the name PLUTO (Pipe-Line Under The Ocean). An engineer of the Anglo-Iranian Oil Company succeeded in creating a 75-mm diameter tube, both sufficiently solid and flexible to be rolled around drums fixed in the

Training in the run-up to D-Day.

Parachute drill for the 6ᵗʰ Airborne.

holds of ships or round gigantic reels floating on the surface of the sea, from which this long tube would be unwound and laid across the bottom of the Channel. Fuel would thus arrive directly on French soil, more rapidly than by a rotation of tankers, and would follow the Allies as they advanced through France, in ordinary pipe-lines.

With regard to an amphibious operation of such magnitude, the question of the landing barges was obviously primordial. In 1940, the British - and the Americans, who were in the same boat – only had a few models, and those were at the experimental stage. Four years later, they had built thousands of barges of 80 different types. Successive landings in the Mediterranean had provided the occasion to develop boats that would satisfy their very diverse requirements: from the enormous transatlantic troop ships, the LSIs (Landing Ship Infantry) to the tiny LCAs (Landing Craft Assault), designed to be launched close to the target shore; there were LCTs (Landing Craft Tanks) used only for vehicles, and LCIs (Landing Craft Infantry) that could carry 200 men over an intermediate distance, to name but a few.

The manufacturers of sewing machines, toys, bath tubs ... switched to the production of the different articles needed in the construction of these thousands of barges. The assembly yards were established close to rivers, in hangars, courtyards, gardens and sometimes even in the roads that ran through even the smallest villages... This is but a fleeting glimpse of the immense war effort that the British people had striven to sustain since 1940. Great Britain had become a throbbing hive of activity.

General Hobart's "Funnies"

Construction of the "Phoenix" caissons for the future artificial ports.

In 1943, however, Great Britain had reached its economic and financial limit. Fortunately, the American giant threw the entire weight of its industrial potential into the equation. Factories on the other side of the Atlantic produced thousands of tanks, lorries, guns, planes (one every five minutes!), a large proportion of which were to find their way across the ocean to accumulate in vast camps, in the run-up to the invasion. In Norfolk House, the COSSAC HQ in St. James' Square, the animation was a miniature reproduction of the activity that had engulfed the whole country. Piles of reports and files on the most diverse subjects, almost all of which were stamped "Top Secret", filled the offices. The models over which the tacticians pored as they developed their plans of action were stored in carefully guarded rooms. Nothing was left to chance. Specialists put photographs of the Normandy coasts, taken almost daily by adventurous planes and submarines, under the microscope, in a meticulous search for the slightest details. The Resistance fighters, for their part, put their lives and freedom on the line,

sending crucially important information on the German defences and troop movements. Thus, nothing of Rommel's considerable efforts to strengthen the beach defences since the beginning of 1944 was unknown to the tacticians. They had an answer to everything! There were specially prepared landing barges. The "Hedgerow" LCTs were designed to launch projectiles at the beach, whose detonation would cause

This giant bobbin was designed for the laying of miles of flexible pipe-line on the ocean floor, part of operation "PLUTO".

A rubber lorry used in the misinformation operation "Fortitude".

A plywood field gun, whose purpose was to fool enemy aerial reconnaissance.

the mines buried in the sand to explode. The terrifying LCT(R), the naval version of the famous "Stalin organs" were equipped with a thousand short-range rockets with a combined detonative power equivalent to 17 tonnes of explosives; they were fired in salvoes and were designed to pulverise everything - obstacles, men and equipment — within an area 700 yards wide and 200 yards deep. For their part, the 79th Armoured Division had been at work developing special tanks for quite some time. On Churchill's orders General Percy

Hobart, its commander, had been brought out of retirement, in which his outspokenness and avant-garde theories had prematurely and inopportunely landed him in 1940. His mission consisted in designing machines capable of both furnishing the infantry with the indispensable and powerful artillery support that had been so cruelly lacking at the tragic incident in Dieppe, and also clearing the beaches of all the different traps and pitfalls that the enemy had put in place. A fantastic gallery of weird-shaped armoured monsters

An inflatable tank.

The massive bombardment of Germany and France was an essential prerequisite for the success of operation Overlord.

was to be born of the fertile imagination deployed by Hobart and his team: this collection of contraptions quickly came to be nicknamed "Funnies" by their detractors, who were numerous until the moment they went into action. The "Petard" tanks carried a large articulated mortar capable of delivering very high explosive charges, nicknamed "flying dustbins", which could take out concrete walls and small blockhouses. The "Crocodiles" were tanks equipped with flame throwers that were so powerful that the infantry's looked like children's toys in comparison. The BARVs (Beach Armoured Recovery Vehicle) and the Tankdozers were charged with unceremoniously clearing away obstacles, be they German, or destroyed or broken down Allied machines, and so avoid the risk of the beaches becoming jammed. The "Crabs", also known as "Flails", carried a drum suspended between two long arms and equipped with chains that lashed the ground to trigger off mines. Audacious sampling missions undertaken by teams of frogmen by night on the Norman shores had indicated that the vehicles would be liable to get bogged down in certain places. Hobart's team dealt with that by inventing the "Bobbin" tank, which was equipped to unroll an extremely tough carpet on which even the heaviest of machines could conserve a perfect manoeuvrability.

Others carried huge bundles of wood designed to fill the anti-tank trenches, and the deep fords, or metal gangways for surmounting anti-tank walls or small rivers. How do you keep a 30-tonne tank afloat in the sea and get it to the shore? An engineer of Hungarian origin, Nicholas Straussler, thought up a bold solution that would certainly have astounded Archimedes himself. A skirt of inflatable canvas, raised and held by a metal frame running around the hull, made completely watertight, would make it possible to transform several hundred Sherman tanks into amphibious machines. In the water, propulsion was by a propeller system. On land, the skirt deflated and the tank could function normally, whence its name "DD" (short for Duplex Drive).

A Stirling bomber on a landing field in England.

The beginning of the countdown

In December 1943, General Dwight Eisenhower was appointed as Supreme Commander in charge of operation Overlord. A mere colonel in 1941, he had spent the major part of his career in staff headquarters, where General Marshall had noticed his talent for organisation. For this reason, he entrusted him with responsibility for the landings in North Africa in November 1942, then operations in Tunisia, during which he had the opportunity of proving himself as a soldier, but also as a diplomat, a quality essential when one is at the head of an army consisting of men of a dozen different nationalities. Three British officers were to second him at the head of the SHAEF (Supreme Headquarters, Allied Expeditionary Force): General Montgomery, in charge of ground troops, Admiral Ramsay from the Navy and Air Marshal Leigh-Mallory in charge of the air force.

In August 1943, General Morgan had had received approval for his plan from the highest Allied authorities in Quebec (the "Quadrant" conference). It provided for three divisions to be landed on the Calvados coast, between Grandcamp and Courseulles, with flanking support from two parachute brigades. When they got wind of the project, Eisenhower and Montgomery judged it to be insufficient and decided to increase the scale of the operation. The invasion would take place along a sector of coast 50 miles long, rather than the initially planned 25 miles, and would include the base of the Cotentin peninsula. It was essential to establish a hold directly in the Manche *département* in the Cotentin in order to capture the port of Cherbourg as quickly as possible.

This modification required more numerous troops: three airborne divisions and five infantry divisions in total. But where would they find the extra barges necessary for the transport of all these supplementary troops? The postponement of the supporting landings in Provence (operation Anvil) until mid-August, which had

A few weeks before the invasion, attacks on the French rail network were stepped up.

originally been planned to take place at the same time as the invasion in Normandy, freed up a certain number. The rest would be supplied by increased productivity; this meant delaying D-Day for a month. The fateful day was thus deferred from the beginning of May to the beginning of June 1944. Taking into account the three principal conditions insisted on by the different people in charge (attack at dawn, after a full-moon night, and on the rising tide), the date settled on was 5th June, with the possibility of hanging fire until the 6th or the 7th.

Since the summer of 1943, the Battle of the Atlantic had changed complexion. Admiral Doenitz' U-boats no longer held sway in the ocean and the Americans could henceforth transport the men and equipment that were to contribute to the success of Overlord to Great Britain. During the first months of 1944, hundreds of thousands of GIs peacefully "invaded" old Albion, accompanied by brand new tanks, lorries and guns that were parked in serried ranks as far as the eye could see across England's green and pleasant land. The countdown had started. From the last months of 1943 on, the strategic bombers bombarded Germany day and night. The objective was not only to destroy its industrial potential, or to terrify the population, but also to constrain the *Luftwaffe* to withdraw the main bulk of its fighters back towards the Reich's territories, thus reducing its capacity to counter-attack in the West when the landings took place.

Operation "Transports" was launched in February 1944, with the aim of destroying the entire rail network and all the rolling stock in north-western France and the surrounding regions. As of April, all the enemy aerodromes within a 125-mile radius of the Channel and North sea coasts were attacked. Then in May it was the coastal batteries' turn. In order not to reveal the place chosen for the assault prematurely, the Allies did their utmost to drop as many bombs on targets situated in the Pas-de-Calais as, if not more than, on those in Normandy. Meanwhile, the troops began to gather in the vast camps in the south of England near the ports whence they were to embark. Even if it was difficult to hide these preparations from the Germans, they could at least be led astray. This was the goal of the misinformation operation "Fortitude". One of its main facets consisted in making their opponent believe that even more troops and equipment had been gathered in south-eastern England, opposite the Pas-de-Calais, than were gathering in the south and west. Moreover, the German high command had been persuaded for many months that the main threat lay there; it was merely a case

Thousands of barges were gathered in the southern English ports.

of flattering their error and prolonging their credulity and the plan's credibility for as long as possible. As they did not have the resources needed to undertake manoeuvres on this scale, the Allies had to develop their talents for weaving illusions. With the wave of a magic wand, hundreds of barges – made of cardboard – jostled in harbours and cluttered up jetties, with the added realism of slicks of fuel oil for effect. Every night, a few convoys of empty lorries, always the same, drove around the region with their headlights on full. In the fields, inflatable tanks were obligingly visible to the snooping enemy spy-planes, which the anti-aircraft defence was under orders to miss, so that they could take their pre-

cious information back to the continent. An entire army was supposed to have set up camp around Dover. The extraordinary radio activity it generated – in reality, fictional exchanges between units that were pure figments of imagination – bore witness to its presence. It was even led by a prestigious figure, General Patton, reputed in German circles to be the most competent of the Anglo-Saxon Generals. They did not know that the ebullient General, who launched himself willy-nilly into the hoax, was in quarantine there, at the head of a phantom army, after his escapades in Sicily. The final phase of the aerial operation, the destruction of the road and rail bridges, began during the last days of May.

The streets of Southampton were overflowing with military vehicles ready to embark.

D-DAY - 2

ALFRED FLETCHER, BBC

IT ALL BEGAN WITH A CALL TO THE ADMIRALTY WHERE, IN A CROWDED CONFERENCE ROOM, THE PRESS LIAISON OFFICER TOLD PRESSMEN AND NEWSREEL MEN FROM THE STATES, CANADA, AUSTRALIA AND BRITAIN THAT THE FIRST ASSAULTS TO PRECEDE THE LIBERATION OF EUROPE WOULD SHORTLY BE UNDER WAY.

THAT FACT LEFT ME A LITTLE INDIFFERENT TO THE REST OF THE BRIEFING AND BACKGROUND – AND THAT WAS IMPRESSIVE ENOUGH. HERE AT LAST, I FELT, WAS THE GREATEST OF ALL TASKS. NOW WE WERE FACE TO FACE WITH THE FACT THAT HISTORY WAS ABOUT TO BE MADE ON A SCALE MORE SHATTERING IN ITS IMPLICATIONS FOR THE FUTURE OF THE WORLD THAN EVER BEFORE. IT WOULD NO LONGER BE SIMPLY "BLOOD, SWEAT, TOIL AND TEARS" BUT INSTEAD THE FIERY SWORD OF VENGEANCE. SOON THE BRIEFING WAS OVER. FEW QUESTIONS WERE ASKED. THERE WAS NOTHING MORE TO SAY. THE REST OF THE DAY, THAT IS TO SAY THE JOURNEY AND THE SUBSEQUENT EMBARKATION, RESOLVED ITSELF INTO A SERIES OF IMPRESSIONS CAUGHT AS WE LUMBERED PAST SUNBATHED FIELDS IN THE MOST UNCOMFORTABLE BUS THE ADMIRALTY COULD FIND. SUNLIT IMPRESSIONS OF WAR - AND PEACE - AND, DESPITE THE LAUGHTER AND THE JOKES THAT ALWAYS FOLLOW MEN AROUND ON THEIR JOURNEYINGS, THAT ONE IMPRESSIVE FACT LOOMING UP AGAIN AND AGAIN: THE SHAPE OF THINGS TO COME. CONTRASTS ALL THE WAY. LIGHT AND SHADE. WAR AND PEACE. HUGE LORRIES DRIVEN BY BULKY BLACK TROOPS AND LITTLE, FLAXEN-HAIRED VILLAGE CHILDREN, SMILING, GRUBBY AND TRANSFIXED WITH SHYNESS INTO COMPLETE DUMBNESS. VAST TANK PARKS, LONG LINES OF LOADED "DUCKS" WITH EVERYTHING ABOARD FROM VALISES TO MOTORCYCLES, JEEPS BY THE MILLION WITH LONG UPWARDS-STICKING SNOUTS TO KEEP THE WATER OUT, VAST CAMOUFLAGED CAMPS, SPRUCE AND ALERT, AND PARKS WITH CHILDREN SPLASHING HAPPILY IN BATHING POOLS. BARBED-WIRE-ENCLOSED WOODS WITH RHODODENDRONS AFLAME, GLIMPSES OF HIDDEN DARK GREEN GUNS, PATHS LEADING TO DUMPS AND, NEARBY, QUIET ENGLISH ROSE GARDENS TO SOOTHE RECUMBENT FIGURES ON STRIPED DECK CHAIRS. THE SCENE CHANGES. ON AND ON PAST THE LONG ROWS – MILE AFTER MILE – OF WEAPONS. TRAFFIC THAT WILL INCREASE BEYOND IMAGINATION DURING THE COMING DAYS. WE REACH BASE. ALL AROUND ME, THE SHIPS OF WAR OF EVERY SHAPE AND SIZE AND COLOUR. COLLEAGUES WHO HAVE FRETTED TO BE OFF FOR WEEKS CLIMB ABOARD LAUNCHES. TENSION RETURNS AND THEY SLIP AWAY WITH A SMILE THAT IS NOT IN THEIR EYES. WE CLAMBER ON DECKS WHERE THERE ARE NO CONTRASTS AND NO DECK CHAIRS.

A column of tanks along a road in Britain, waiting to embark for Normandy.

"OK, We'll go!"

On the evening of 2nd June, the warships left their bases in Scapa Flow, Belfast, and the Clyde to sail down the Irish Sea. The next day, the boarding of troops began in the southern ports, which were full to the gunwales. As the cranes took the strain, the men, packs on backs and in long lines, followed instructions coming from loudspeakers and moved to their designated places. The most massive war machine ever gathered was in motion. Eisenhower had moved his headquarters to Southwick House, a large Georgian mansion near Portsmouth, a few weeks previously. Twice daily, the staff met in the library for conferences exclusively consecrated to the weather forecasts. In May, the weather had been ideal. Unfortunately, in the first days of June, it deteriorated. A stiff westerly breeze blew up and the waves began to form crests. On Sunday 4th June at 04h15 in the morning, half a dozen men were hanging on the words of a dry, austere Scot, Group Captain Stagg. His forecast for 5th June was very pessimistic: "Rough sea, poor visibility and low cloud". The invasion was put back at least 24 hours and the first troop ships, which were already at sea, were hastily recalled. A new element was considered at the conference held that evening at 9 o'clock. Stagg forecast a period of relative calm on the 6th, based on observations made in the North Atlantic. The final decision was deferred until the small hours of the following morning. Monday 5th June, 4 o'clock in the morning. Whereas a stormy wind was blowing, and heavy rain was falling on Southwick House, Stagg confirmed his forecast: favourable weather for the morning of the 6th. After having quickly gone round the table, Eisenhower took the most important decision of his entire existence. It was delivered with few words: "OK, we'll go!" Before going back to his caravan in the grounds, he drafted a brief communiqué.: *"Our landings in the Cherbourg-Le Havre area have failed to gain a satisfactory foothold, and I have had to withdraw our troops. My decision to attack at this point and at this moment were based on the most reliable evidence at my disposal. The army, the navy and the air force did all that bravery and devotion to duty could do. If any blame is attached to the event, it is mine alone."* He was to discover this sombre message, forgotten in one of his pockets, several weeks after the landings.

Equipment parks sprawled across the landscape.

En route
for Normandy

TUESDAY 6TH JUNE 1944

"Under the command of General Eisenhower Allied naval forces supported by strong air forces began landing Allied armies this morning on the northern coast of France."

Communiqué N° 1 by the SHAEF, broadcast by the BBC on 6th June 1944 at 09h30 a.m.

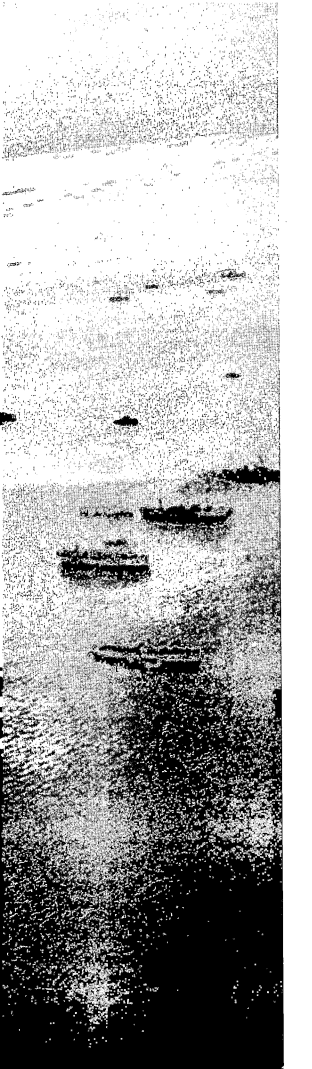

THOUSANDS OF BOATS OFF THE NORMANDY COAST

Under cover of night, the immense Allied armada sailed quietly to within a few miles of the Normandy shore, where they moored fore and aft without the enemy noticing. This was not the least of the exploits achieved that historic day. *"We benefited from an element of surprise that we had never dared hope for,"* as Eisenhower said later. The ships left harbours in Cornwall, Devon, the Solent and Sussex in their thousands during the morning and the afternoon of 5th June. They all converged on zone "Z", the assembly point south of the Isle of Wight, that soon came to be known as *"Piccadilly Circus"*, because the congestion there was no less dense than that characteristic of the famous London junction's rush-hour traffic jam. Thence, they left in five convoys, each in the direction of the assault sector it had been assigned to. The sea was rough. All night, the endless stream of ships heavily laden with men and equipment sailed south in tight formation, to the point that bows sometimes collided with the sterns in front of them.

Thousands of boats of all sizes were assembled off the coast.

Prayer before the assault on a Canadian troop carrier.

Amongst them, some old ships were on their last voyage. They were to be scuppered offshore, and their hulks were to become protection from the waves for the anchorages and artificial harbours to come. This was to be the fate of the venerable French battleship Courbet after thirty three-years of good and faithful service. The immense armada advanced at the same careful pace as the minesweepers that opened the way before them. On its flanks, high speed corvettes equipped with loud-speakers tirelessly powered to and fro like so many sheepdogs. How could this gigantic merry-go-round have escaped the German' notice? The *Kriegsmarine*, lulled into a false sense of security by the bad weather, had renounced sending its usual patrols out into the Channel that night. For the same reason, the *Luftwaffe* did not consider it worthwhile to organise any reconnaissance sorties. Around 3 o'clock in the morning, when the first parachute drops were reported, Admiral Hennécke sent several fast launches out from Cherbourg. They soon returned, over-awed by the storm, and without having seen anything.

As for the 90 coastal radar stations in the Channel sector, they had nearly all been destroyed by the Allied aviation during the days and weeks preceding the assault, thus blinding the enemy's detection systems. Those that had escaped destruction were jammed by powerful interference from the systems that had been installed on over two hundred and fifty ships. Only a few tracking stations north of the Seine had been left intact: voluntarily, as they were to be the unwitting participants in a mystification exercise. As the invasion fleet was nearing its destination, two strange convoys were making for Le Havre and Calais: a few motor launches towing balloons equipped with reflectors behind them were to create a series of hits on the radar screens and create the illusion of a large fleet heading for the Pas-de-Calais. For the same purpose, bomber squadrons scattered chaff, a profusion of pieces of aluminium foil, while night fighters flew over the Picardy coast in ceaseless rotation.

While the Germans were busy trying to find the phantom army, they completely forgot about the Seine Bay, which the real invaders managed to reach without hindrance. The only hitch occurred about 5 o'clock in the morning, on the invasion force's left flank. Three torpedo boats, under the command of Corvette Captain Hoffmann, suddenly appeared from out of the smokescreen hiding the armada from the coastal batteries in Le Havre, to discover the incredible sight of the Allied armada peacefully making its way through the water. Once the torpedo boats had fired their torpedoes blind, the assailants disappeared back into the mist out of which they had come, and as quickly. The Allied ships nimbly manoeuvred to avoid the danger. One torpedo, however, ended up hitting the Norwegian destroyer Svenner, which sank immediately. This was the sole appearance and intervention by the *Kriegsmarine* during the landings. Too little and too late to turn the tide of history. As the night receded, and the first light of dawn began to creep across the sky, the sea was literally covered, from the mouth of the Seine to the Cotentin, in ships and boats of all sizes

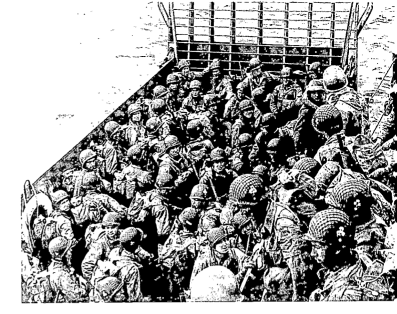

Embarking onto the barges. Objective: Utah Beach.

ranging from the biggest battleships to the smallest landing barges. How many were there? Hundreds; thousands. On shore, the Germans, stuck in their concrete shelters away from the bombs that continued to rain down on them, did not have the time nor the leisure to count them. Shortly after 5 o'clock in the morning the medium and heavy bombers of the US Air Force took over from the RAF aircraft. And then the fleet opened fire, unleashing the tremendous power of its big guns. The first assault craft were already making a bee-line for the coast. The first phase of operation Overlord, operation Neptune, the amphibious assault, had begun.

A squadron of Boston bombers flying over the invasion fleet. The black and white stripes on the wings simplified the identification of Allied aircraft.

Mer of the Royal Winnipeg Rifles heading for Courseulles and Graye on board their LCAs (Landing Craft Assault).

TODAY'S THE DAY

COLIN WILLS, BBC

THIS IS THE DAY AND THIS IS THE HOUR. THE SKY IS LIGHTENING OVER
THE COAST OF EUROPE AS WE GO IN.
THE SKY IS LIGHTER AND THE SEA IS BRIGHTER, BUT ALONG THE
SHORE THERE IS A DENSE SMOKESCREEN, AS THE BATTLESHIPS AND
THE WARSHIPS, THE SMALLER WARSHIPS, SWEEP ALONG THERE,
FIRING ALL THE TIME AGAINST THE SHORE, SOME OF THEM LAYING A
SMOKESCREEN FOR US. THE SUN IS BLAZING DOWN BRIGHTLY NOW. IT'S
ALMOST LIKE AN OMEN, THE WAY IT'S SUDDENLY COME OUT, JUST AS
WE ARE GOING IN. THE WHOLE SKY IS BRIGHT, THE SEA IS A GLITTER-
ING MASS OF SILVER, AS CRAFT OF EVERY KIND MOVE ACROSS IT, THE
GREAT BATTLESHIPS IN THE BACKGROUND BLAZING AWAY AT THE
SHORE. THERE GO THE LANDING CRAFT. SOME ARE LEFT BEHIND – THE
SLOWER ONES. EACH TAKING THEIR PART AND GOING IN AT THE RIGHT
TIME FOR THE RIGHT JOB. DESTROYERS, CORVETTES, PATROL VES-
SELS... I CAN HEAR THE SOUND OF ANTI-AIRCRAFT FIRE. I CAN'T SEE
YET WHETHER IT'S OUR PEOPLE BEING ATTACKED. THERE'S AN ENOR-
MOUS CLOUD OF SMOKE ALONG THE SHORE, NOT ONLY FROM THE
SMOKESCREEN, BUT ALSO FROM THE TERRIFIC BOMBARDMENT. ALL
THE SHIPS ARE BLAZING AWAY NOW, ALL AROUND US, IN A GIGANTIC
CIRCLE, THERE ARE SHIPS. SHIPS MOVING IN, SHIPS ON PATROL, SHIPS
CIRCLING, SHIPS STANDING TO AND FIRING. WE'RE PASSING CLOSE BY
A CRUISER, A CRUISER THAT HAS BEEN TAKING PART IN THE BOM-
BARDMENT BUT IS NOW, I IMAGINE, A SORT OF GENERAL PATROL.
YOU CAN'T IMAGINE ANYTHING LIKE THIS MARCH OF SHIPS, LIKE SOL-
DIERS MARCHING IN LINE. I'VE NEVER SEEN ANYTHING SO EXPRESSIVE
OF INTENSE PURPOSE. IT'S A PURPOSE SHARED AMONG MANY SHIPS
AND AMONG MANY HUNDREDS OF THOUSANDS OF FIGHTING MEN.
THEY'RE DRAWING IN NOW TO THE COAST OF EUROPE TO DO THE BIG-
GEST JOB THEY'VE EVER HAD TO DO...
I CAN'T KEEP YOU ANY MORE NOW, BECAUSE THE TIME HAS COME FOR
ME TO GET MY KIT ON MY BACK AND GET READY TO STEP OVER ON
THAT SHORE. AND IT'S A GREAT DAY.

"H" HOUR
ON UTAH BEACH

4.00

As of 4 o'clock in the morning, the men in the first assault waves left the large troop ships and boarded the smaller assault craft, LCAs or LCMs, pitching and yawing roughly in the heavy swell. Real "floating shoeboxes". Many of the soldiers were grey and pasty-faced. They were suffering from cold and cramps. Some had already spent over two days in stinking holds, and it showed. Above all, they had to fight against merciless and horrible sea-sickness. The pills they had been given for this purpose had had very little positive effect, and most of the soldiers were reduced to using the brown paper bags they had been so generously offered.

They clambered down the netting and crouched in the bottom of the fragile craft without a word, trying to shelter from the driving spray that soaked their combat dress. They slid sheaths over their rifle barrels to avoid the ravages of the salt water. This had caused a lot of laughter during training, but the time for joking was now past.

Men and equipment landing without much difficulty on the beach down from the dunes at La Madeleine.

At 04h55, twenty landing barges carrying 600 men of the 8th American Infantry Regiment set out for Utah Beach, 10 nautical miles away on the eastern side of the Cotentin. Their mission was to conquer the terrain where General Barton's 4th Infantry Division was to land. The flotilla was escorted by support ships, notably LCTs carrying "DD" amphibious tanks, which it was planned to launch one and a half miles offshore. The trip was long, lasting an hour and a half, and finished the job of emptying even the most resistant stomachs.

5:40

At 05h40 a frightful din burst in their ears. The fleet had just opened fire, simultaneously spitting shells from every one of its guns in a deafening concert. The projectiles whistled high overhead and smashed into the coast, where yellowish geysers spurted up from the beaches. The naval bombardment lasted three-quarters of an hour without respite. It was complemented by the intervention of the 9th US Air Force's Marauders, which poured 4,400 tonnes of bombs on the German defences.

5h45: the fleet opened fire. The battleship USS Nevada, an escapee from Pearl Harbor, hurling its 356-mm projectiles at the Azeville and Saint-Marcouf batteries.

6:31

Land was approaching. Through the unbelievable clouds of smoke and dust that were hanging over the shore, the officers began trying to make out landmarks that had become familiar during their repeated scrutiny of maps and photographs. The LCT(R)s belched out their devastating salvoes of rockets in a cacophony of strident whistling. Finally, the P-47 Thunderbolt fighter-bombers attacked the coastal positions with rockets to finish them off. When they were 400 yards from their objective, the leading barges launched smoke bombs. This was the agreed signal for the navy to cease firing. It was 06h31, "H" hour to within a minute.

The 4th Division landing on Utah Beach.

Near Saint-Marie-du-Mont. These Georgians of the 795th Osttruppen Battalion have just surrendered to the Americans.

The engines were cut. The barges' momentum took them gently scraping over the sandy sea bottom. The ramps were lowered. The men leapt into cold water up to their waists. Not pleasant. The weather was still overcast. Decidedly, there was nothing radiant about this Tuesday 6th June.

Each one did their best to advance as quickly as possible, in spite of the weight of their legs, made leaden by the resistance of the water. They clenched their teeth as they thought of the enemy who must be watching them from over there, fingers on triggers. Dry land at last. In spite of their exhaustion, the assault waves surged up to the dunes. They took some time to realise that, opposite them, resistance was weak; there were a few detonations, but not much sustained firing. Stunned by the deluge of bombs and shells that had just stopped raining down on their positions, the sector's defenders had hardly had the time to get their wits back about them.

Some didn't even try to shoot at the assailants. White flags sprang up here and there. A few more determined men tried to repel the attack, but the abrupt appearance of the amphibious tanks, careering out of the water like enraged sea monsters as they fired on the few recalcitrant fortified positions, put paid to what morale they had left, and to the remaining pockets of resistance. The units in front drove inland without hesitating, following the raised causeways running through the flooded areas behind the dunes. During this time, specialised teams cleared the beach of obstacles and opened breaches in the anti-tank wall to facilitate the arrival of the in-coming units and heavy equipment that would not really be bothered by the somewhat sporadic enemy fire. The landing on Utah Beach was not exactly a party, but at least it was accomplished with surprising ease. The Americans lost less than 50 men. General Theodore Rooosevelt, lieutenant-commander of the 4th Division, who came in with the first wave of assailants, was not slow to comprehend. The strong off-shore wind and the powerful coastal currents had led his troops to land at La Madeleine, in the commune of Sainte-Marie-du-Mont, about 1 1/2 miles south of the intended place, in a sector that was less well defended than the Varreville sector, and out of range of the coastal batteries in Morsalines and Azeville.

A German soldier killed during the assault.

First aid.

The battery at Saint-Marcouf (Crisbec), which was more powerful, was too involved in duelling with the fleet to target the beach more than occasionally. Navigational errors are rarely so providential!

BLOODY OMAHA

Whereas the landing on Utah Beach was accomplished without meeting any real resistance, the situation was very different on the other American beach, just a few miles away.

Omaha Beach was a long curving shore about five miles long, bordered by a very steep escarpment and closed at both extremities by cliffs rising 100 feet above the sea. In order to reach the plateau, where lay the villages of Colleville, Vierville and Saint-Laurent, the troops would have to climb four deeply cleft ravines that were easy for the defenders to block. As it happened, the Germans had indeed taken advantage of the topography by studding the area with artillery pillboxes, machine-gun and mortar trenches that covered the beach. In short, a veritable trap for the men of the 1st and 29th American Infantry Divisions! But the Allies had no choice. There was nowhere else between Arromanches and the Vire estuary that lent itself to the landing of troops, and it was unthinkable to leave a yawning gap in the assault sector between Utah beach and the beaches that devolved on the British.

The arrival of the second assault wave of the 16th Infantry Regiment.

When the second wave of assault came into Omaha Beach just before 7 o'clock, it was welcomed by abnormally intense firing. Bullets ricocheted off the barges' landing ramps. All around them, spurts of machine gun fire sent up sprays of water and fountains of sand. They were soon to understand the magnitude of their predicament. The first wave had been literally nailed to the spot. Dozens of bodies already slopped lifelessly in the choppy waves and backwash. The beach was littered with ruination, smoking wreckage, debris, abandoned weapons and inert cadavers. A few hundred yards in front of them they could see the survivors, huddled under the providential shelter provided by the pebble levee. Others had hastily dug themselves into the sand, heads hunched down between their shoulders. All the units were mixed up and completely disorientated, most of them having lost their officers; a shambles of a mass of individuals more preoccupied with saving their own skins than with capturing enemy positions. The roles had been exchanged: the assailants had no thoughts other than for their own survival. Whereas the men of the 29th Division were experiencing their - tragic - baptism by fire, the soldiers of the 1st Division, the famous Big Red One, were battle-hardened

The first waves of assault, pinned down and sheltering behind the obstacles erected by the Germans.

veterans of combat in North Africa and in Sicily. For all their experience, they were just as impotent as their comrades, victims of an incredible and unfavourable combination of circumstances. It was to come to light later that the GIs had not been up against the mediocre regiment of ageing has-beens who it was thought were guarding the zone, but General Kraiss' 352nd Infantry Division, a perfectly trained and well equipped unit, which had been stationed there just a few weeks previously, without London getting wind of their arrival. To cap this stroke of bad luck, the German defences had miraculously escaped all the bombardments due to poor visibility. The clusters of missiles launched by the B 24 Liberators had gone ploughing inland, up to three miles from the shore. The rocket salvoes fired by the LCT(R)s had fallen short, into the sea, and only served to massacre several thousand fish which the invaders found floating belly-up on the water's surface. And finally, the naval barrage had not been as efficient as usual. The German bunkers' slits opened onto the beach, and not on the sea and so only their thick concrete flanks had been exposed to the shells from the battleships Texas and Arkansas and the French cruisers Montcalm and Georges Leygues.

The evacuation of the wounded.

Finally, on the beach, support from armour was cruelly lacking. Half of the 64 "DD" amphibious tanks assigned to the sector were launched much too far out, over three miles from the shore, in high seas. All but two of them sank pretty much straight away. As a precaution, the second group was landed directly on the beach, but much later; too late. Many of the over-laden amphibious DUCKW trucks were swamped and capsized, sending the precious 105-mm Howitzers and the heavy equipment so badly needed by the infantry to the sea-bed.

On Omaha, the carnage did not stop. The second wave, caught in its turn in the enemy cross-fire, took a severe thrashing. The men ran, stumbled, fell, picked themselves up... or lay still forever. Other barges arrived in the midst of an indescribable chaos and ran into a new danger. The tide was rising and had begun covering the obstacles on the beach that had not been cleared away; the demolition teams entrusted with this mission had been decimated under the withering defensive fire and the Americans had made the mistake of turning down the British offers of General Hobart's special contraptions.

Boats collided in their attempts to avoid the traps. Others were impaled or exploded on the mines attached to by now partially hidden stakes. Confusion reigned supreme.

Men jumped into water up to their necks and did not dare to leave it, believing themselves to be safer in deep water. Others took refuge behind semi-submerged "hedgehogs". The war correspondent Frank Capa took photos from the beach, immortalising the tragic Omaha episode. At the eastern extremity of Omaha, on Fox Red, traumatised men found blessed shelter at the foot of the cliffs. The tide went on rising inexorably, drowning the wounded men abandoned to their fate and reducing the narrow strip of sand, stranded men and equipment caught in its noose, to a mere spit. Boats circled off the beach, unable to get close to the shore, which was by now totally saturated, and provided sitting ducks for the adversary, whose ardour was unabated. On board the cruiser Augusta General Bradley, commander-in-chief of the American troops, received a constant stream of alarming reports from Omaha.

At 08h30 he first decided to delay the departure of the following waves. Then he considered sending them to Utah or the British beaches. He was still wondering what to do when, towards the end of the morning, he at last received an encouraging message. Some of his men had succeeded in getting out of the tight corner they had been stuck in for seven hours. The destroyers had moved as close to the shore as possible and had recommenced firing on the German defences. They began to weaken. On land, a few energetic leaders, such

The German 352nd Division in charge of the Omaha sector put up fierce resistance

as Colonel Taylor, had taken the situation in hand. The famous shout: *"There are two types of men who will stay on this beach: the dead and those who are going to die. Let's get out of here!"* is attributed to him. On their last legs, and inch by inch, ignoring the over-well defended entrances to the ravines, the GIs began scaling the long embankment and managed to find their way onto the plateau at the top, through mines and barbed wire. The first ones there made it for midday, and began attacking the Germans from behind. The advantage changed hands. But at what a price! All told, there were 4,000 dead and seriously wounded in the American ranks. Success was not yet certain, but disaster had been avoided. The invasion very nearly met a tragic end here on the bloody beach of Omaha.

Two soldiers inspecting one of the bunkers (this one was equipped with an 88-mm gun) that caused such heavy losses in the American ranks.

Bloody Omaha

Identifying the bodies on Dog White, evening of 6ᵗʰ June.

THE FLOTSAM AND JETSAM OF WAR

ERNIE PYLE, WAR CORRESPONDENT FOR NUMEROUS AMERICAN PUBLICATIONS

I TOOK A WALK ALONG THE HISTORIC COAST OF NORMANDY IN THE COUNTRY OF FRANCE. IT WAS A LOVELY DAY FOR STROLLING ALONG THE SEASHORE. MEN WERE SLEEPING ON THE SAND, SOME OF THEM SLEEPING FOREVER. MEN WERE FLOATING IN THE WATER, BUT THEY DIDN'T KNOW THEY WERE IN THE WATER, FOR THEY WERE DEAD. THE WRECKAGE WAS VAST AND STARTLING. YOU COULD SEE TRUCKS TIPPED OVER AND SWAMPED. YOU COULD SEE PARTLY SUNKEN BARGES, AND THE ANGLED-UP CORNERS OF JEEPS, AND SMALL LANDING CRAFT HALF SUBMERGED. ON THE BEACH ITSELF, HIGH AND DRY, WERE ALL KINDS OF WRECKED VEHICLES. THERE WERE TANKS THAT HAD ONLY JUST MADE THE BEACH BEFORE BEING KNOCKED OUT. THERE WERE JEEPS THAT HAD BURNED TO A DULL GREY. THERE WERE BOATS STACKED ON TOP OF EACH OTHER, THEIR SIDES CAVED IN, THEIR SUSPENSION DOORS KNOCKED OFF. IN THE WATER FLOATED EMPTY LIFE RAFTS AND SOLDIERS' PACKS AND RATION BOXES AND MYSTERIOUS ORANGES.

BUT THERE WAS OTHER, MORE HUMAN WRECKAGE. THERE WAS A THIN LINE SEVERAL MILES LONG THAT LOOKED LIKE THE LINE OF SEAWEED LEFT BY THE HIGH TIDE. IT WAS THE PERSONAL BELONGINGS OF THE SOLDIERS THAT HAD BEEN SCATTERED THERE; EQUIPMENT THAT THOSE WHO HAD FOUGHT AND DIED DURING THE LANDING WOULD NO LONGER NEED.

THERE WERE BAGS, SOCKS, SHOE POLISH, SEWING KITS, NOTEBOOKS, LETTERS. THERE WERE TOOTHBRUSHES, RAZORS, FAMILY SNAPSHOTS WHOSE IMMOBILE GAZE ROSE UP OUT OF THE SAND TO MEET US. THERE WERE WALLETS, METAL MIRRORS, TROUSERS, ABANDONED AND BLOODY SHOES. THERE WERE SPADES WITH BROKEN HAFTS, SMASHED TRANSISTOR RADIOS, AND BENT AND USELESS MINE DETECTORS. THERE WERE TORN REVOLVER BELTS, CANVAS BUCKETS, INDIVIDUAL PACKETS OF BANDAGES, BIG STACKS OF THROWN-AWAY LIFE-BELTS. I PICKED UP A POCKET BIBLE; IT HAD A SOLDIER'S NAME INSIDE. I CARRIED IT FOR HALF A MILE, THEN I PUT IT BACK DOWN ON THE BEACH. I DON'T KNOW WHY I PICKED IT UP, NOR WHY I PUT IT BACK DOWN. SOLDIERS CARRY STRANGE THINGS WITH THEM. IN EVERY INVASION, THERE IS ALWAYS A SOLDIER LANDING AT "H" HOUR WITH A BANJO OVER HIS SHOULDER. THE MOST IRONIC OBJECT IN ALL THIS MESS WAS A TENNIS RACQUET THAT A SOLDIER HAD BROUGHT WITH HIM. IT LAY ALL ALONE IN THE SAND, TIGHT IN ITS PRESS, NOT A STRING BROKEN.

THE THING WE SAW MOST IN THE DEBRIS WERE CIGARETTES AND WRITING PAPER. THE MEN HAD INTENDED TO WRITE A LOT WHILE IN FRANCE. LETTERS THAT WOULD NOW NEVER BE WRITTEN AND THAT WOULD HAVE FILLED ALL THOSE ABANDONED BLANK PAGES.

THE STRONG AND SWIRLING TIDAL CURRENTS ON THE NORMANDY COAST MODIFIED THE BEACH'S CONTOURS AS THEY EBBED AND FLOWED. THEY CARRIED THE SOLDIERS' BODIES OUT TO SEA AND LATER BROUGHT THEM BACK AGAIN. THEY COVERED THE HEROES' BODIES WITH SAND AND, AT THEIR WHIM, UNCOVERED THEM AGAIN. AS I PROGRESSED WITH DIFFICULTY OVER THE WET SAND, I SKIRTED AROUND SOMETHING THAT SEEMED TO ME LIKE TWO WOODEN WRECKS STICKING OUT OF THE SAND. BUT IT WASN'T A WRECK. IT WAS A SOLDIER'S TWO FEET. HE WAS ALMOST ENTIRELY COVERED IN SAND. ONLY HIS FEET WERE UNCOVERED. THE TIPS OF HIS SHOES WERE POINTING TOWARDS THE LAND THAT HE HAD COME SO FAR TO SEE, AND THAT HE HAD SEEN SO FLEETINGLY.

THE HEROIC ASSAULT ON THE POINTE DU HOC

The most spectacular episode of a day full of such events

happened three and a half miles west of Omaha Beach, at

the Pointe du Hoc. The Germans had installed an impres-

sive battery of six 155-mm guns in bunkers and pillboxes

on a promontory that rose 100 feet vertically from the

sea. Their range, about 12 miles, meant that they covered

both Utah and Omaha sectors, respectively to the west

and to the east. Consequently, they represented a terrible

threat for the American soldiers. Of course, the position

had been copiously showered with bombs during the days

leading up to D-Day, but the result of this aerial bom-

bardment was not known, and prudence dictated that

the position should be captured as quickly as possible.

This was the mission entrusted to the 2nd Ranger

Battalion, an elite troop led by Lieutenant-Colonel James

Rudder, an accomplished and strapping 34-year-old

athlete. His men were to land at the foot of the cliff, scale

it, capture the battery and destroy the guns. They had

spent a long time training on the Isle of Wight,

developing the necessary techniques and equipment.

*A small landslide caused by a naval shell made the climb of some of
the Rangers easier.*

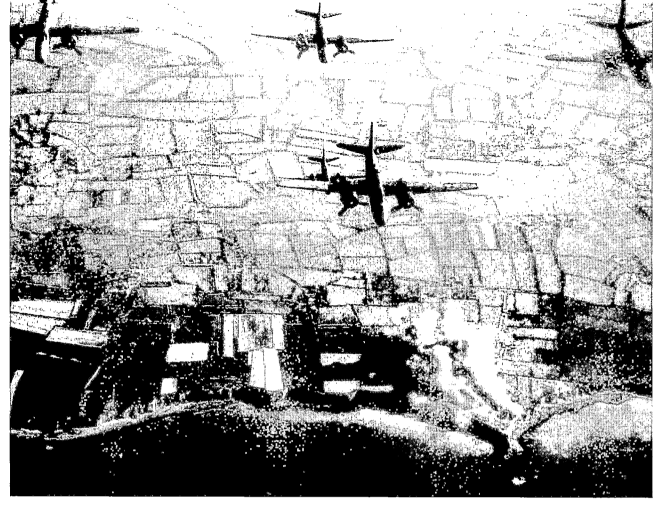

4th June 1944. A squadron of the 9th US Air Force's A-20 bombers over the Pointe du Hoc.

On 6th June about 6 o'clock in the morning, as a pale sun was rising, a small flotilla of 12 LCA barges and 4 amphibious DUCKW trucks carrying the 230 Rangers and their equipment was advancing towards its objective with difficulty. There was a heavy swell and big waves washed over the barges, one of which sank leaving only one survivor. The men in the other boats who witnessed the drama began bailing with their helmets with redoubled energies for fear of meeting the same fate; that did not prevent another boat from sinking in its turn.

There was the coast. To their stupefaction, the objective they were approaching was not the right one. The pilots, who had been swept off course by the current, had mistaken the Pointe de la Percée, three miles to the east, for the Pointe du Hoc. They had to about turn and sail along the coast. This error delayed the operation by about 40 minutes: the consequences were potentially catastrophic. The naval barrage had ceased at 06h30, the assigned time for the assault, and the enemy had had enough time to reorganise. As they approached their goal, a shell scored a direct hit on a DUCKW. The Rangers could see Germans at the top of the cliffs, who began firing at them with rifles and machine guns. Fifteen of the Rangers were taken out as the unit left the barges and struggled to the foot of the cliff, sometimes falling up to their necks in the post-bombardment under-water craters around the site. For the same reason, the DUCKWs became stuck and could not come sufficiently close to make proper use of the fireman's ladders they were equipped with.

One audacious soldier even climbed to the top of one of these ladders, grabbed the machine guns fixed to the top of it and fired spurts at the cliff top... while trying to avoid falling off his uncomfortable perch, which was pitching violently under the effect of the waves. Fortunately, the destroyers Talybont and Satterlee drew as close inshore as their draught would allow and began copiously showering the Germans with their cannons and heavy machine-guns, forcing them into a temporary retreat. The grapnel launchers fixed to the rails of the LCAs went into action, but the water had made the ropes very heavy. Some remained stuck in their boxes. Others reached their target, but many fell back down or caught too far down the cliff face. No matter, the climb began all over the cliff face and using whatever means was available. Some intrepid men even tried climbing using their bare hands and bayonets planted into the rock face. The portable grapnel launchers carried to the base of the cliff proved to be more effective. The Germans, who were back on the edge of the cliff-top, threw grenades down at them, fired machine pistols and cut the ropes. Men slid down the wet rock face, grazing themselves as they fell, in some instances very heavily. Others were luckier: a shell hit the cliff and caused a minor landslide. The resulting pile of boulders and earth reduced the distance they had to climb by half. The best climbers made it to the top in a matter of minutes. When they got there, they discovered a landscape straight from the pages of the

A poor quality but very rare document: two Rangers posing on one of the guns found over half a mile from the Pointe du Hoc.

Hidden in a sunken lane, one of the famous guns from the Pointe du Hoc, which had been moved after the bombardment on 15th April 1944.

apocalypse: a labyrinth of craters pockmarked the ground; destroyed paths and trenches surrounded artillery positions and shelters that were covered with earth, twisted metal and concrete debris, and destroyed by the bombs and shells to varying degrees. They were joined in under half an hour by nearly all of the 170 or 180 Rangers still fit to fight. Colonel Rudder installed his HQ between the cliff-top and one of the bunkers captured by his men. In fact, this first part of the mission, the most spectacular and a priori the most perilous, was to have resulted in much less loss of life than anticipated. The next part of the operation was to be considerably more murderous. First, there were the long hours of combat to clean up the area. Leaping from crater to crater, the Rangers did their best to accomplish the precise missions they were given. One group attacked the firing command post, which was still intact, with bazookas and grenades, yet did not manage to capture it. To their amazement, others finally discovered the remains of the gun silos in this lunar wasteland, only to find them empty. The famous guns, whose capture had led the Rangers into one of the craziest escapades of D-Day, were no longer there.

In accordance with orders, several detachments set off immediately in the direction of the road from Vierville to Grandcamp, in order to cut off the German reinforcements that would be heading for Omaha. They got there at 8 o'clock, not without some losses, and established a defensive perimeter behind the thick Norman hedges. One hour later, pushing forward on the trail of some enigmatic tracks in the earth, a patrol

grenades, before blowing up the stocks of munitions. On site on the Point itself, the struggle went on. The Germans made use of the remaining trenches and underground galleries to pop up unexpectedly here and there and shoot at the Rangers. During these sporadic, brief but violent confrontations, many Americans were killed or wounded, or taken prisoner. Others fell to snipers. Artillery fire from inland added to the toll

Rangers in action.

discovered the guns in question, ready to fire, with munitions close at hand, round the corner of a lane; their operating teams were nowhere to be seen. It was later to come to light that the battery commander had decided to shelter the five remaining cannons, after one had been destroyed in the first bombardment of the Pointe du Hoc on 15th April 1944. The guns were never installed in the two finished bunkers for lack of adequate gun carriages. Without further ado, the Rangers rendered the guns definitively useless by destroying the breech loading mechanisms with thermite

of victims. After several vain attempts, Colonel Rudder finally managed to get a radio message through, around midday: *"Pointe du Hoc – mission accomplished – need munitions and reinforcements – heavy losses."* The answer was not very encouraging. "No reinforcements available – all the Rangers have landed." Because of the delayed start to the assault, and the absence of information, the general staff had redirected the reserve troops to Omaha beach, believing the operation to be a failure.

From that moment on, Colonel Rudder's position and

A first aid post established in a crater.

that of his men became particularly precarious. Whereas the fighting was not even finished right inside the battery, the German reinforcements launched several counter offensives during the afternoon. They were repelled using mortars and machine guns. During the night of 6th − 7th June, more attacks on the defensive perimeter established south of the Vierville-Grandcamp road obliged the Rangers, who were submerged, to fall back towards the tip of the Point, with heavy losses. Their situation had become critical.

Colonel Rudder set up his command post at the edge of the cliff. The American flag was to ward off any misplaced air strikes by Allied aircraft.

A soldier examining the bunker destroyed by the bombardment on 15th April 1944, after the battle. The gun had been overturned by the blast.

GOLD BEACH:
A BRITISH REVENGE

"H" hour had been set at 07h30 for the assault sectors assigned to the British army, due to the difference in tide times. British and Canadian troops were to land on the Calvados coast between Asnelles and Ouistreham, at the mouth of the Orne, on three beaches code-named Gold, Juno and Sword. For many of them, this 6th June 1944 had the sweetness of revenge. This date was to efface the humiliations suffered in Dunkirk and Dieppe. They had been training hard in camps in Great Britain, or in the sands of the Libyan desert, for four years. Since 1940 the particularly anglophile Normans had been hoping for their return to the continent. In spite of all its efforts, Nazi propaganda had not succeeded in turning public opinion against them, despite the unscrupulous and shameless use of arguments such as Mers el-Kebir, in spite of the memory of Joan of Arc, "*burned alive at the stake in Rouen*", or of Napoleon, "*who died in exile in Saint Helena*". Here at last were the Tommies, with their familiar silhouette, and funny wash basin-shaped helmets on their heads.

In Arromanches, the village grocer had a good bottle ready for the liberators.

Aerial view of the King Green sector at Ver-sur-Mer. Infantry transport ships preparing to land.

Their task was not an easy one. The shores of the Calvados were protected by many strong points, operational bases, and fortified positions, containing anti-tank guns, and machine-gun trenches. The sea-front villas, whose inhabitants had long since been kicked out, had become ideal firing positions. The beaches were covered with a multitude of obstacles and their access roads were blocked by walls or anti-tank trenches. The coastal villages' streets had been blocked here and there with barbed wire and concrete walls to create a labyrinth for the purpose of hindering the progress of men and tanks. In short, the charming little seaside towns on the Côte de Nacre now had the unwelcoming aspect of entrenched camps. Gold Beach was the sector assigned to General Graham's British 50th Division. This battle-hardened unit had been the last to leave the beaches at Dunkirk in 1940, before distinguishing itself at El-Alamein, in Tunisia and in Sicily. The shore at Asnelles and Ver-sur-Mer, partially composed of dunes and marsh, was par-

ticularly well defended at its two extremities, around the hamlets of La Rivière and Le Hamel. Further inland, the two batteries in La Mare Fontaine and Le Mont Fleury stood guard over the coast; further west there were two more, one at Vaux and the other at Longues, between Arromanches and Port-en-Bessin, without doubt the most formidable, with its four 150-mm guns well protected by their bunkers. The British, enlightened by their traumatic experience during the raid on Dieppe, were more cautious than the Americans, and decided to send their special armour onto the beaches at the same time as their first waves of infantry. This was a wise precaution as, just like the amphibious "DD" tanks, they were to be of vital importance in the final reckoning. German resistance was robust around the village of Le Hamel at the western end of the sector. It prevented the invading forces from making any inroads towards Arromanches for long hours, and made the destruction of the obstacles on the beach by the teams of

Royal Engineers very perilous. To make matters worse, the tide was rising much faster than had been anticipated. In the middle of the beach, fortunately, the British easily defeated the mediocre Osttruppen stationed there: most of them ran away without further ado, or simply surrendered. The next step was to cross the minefield in the marshes on the other side of the coast road. The "*Crab*" tanks moved into action. Furiously lashing the ground in front of them with their flails, in a concert of detonations, they cleared paths through the fields, opening routes far inland for the infantry and armour, thus initiating the overwhelming of the Le Hamel position by the south. Meanwhile, at the eastern end of Gold Beach, the operational bases in the La Rivière hamlet had fallen and the Green Howards regiment had captured the two batteries in Ver, whose operators had been severely affected by the air strikes and naval shelling, without too much difficulty. Throughout the afternoon, the British troops moved through the Norman countryside

A column of the "Northumbrian" penetrating inland.

towards Bayeux and the RN13 (the main road between Caen and Bayeux). After having captured Crepon, they had some difficulty repelling a German counter-attack between Villers-le-Sec and Bazenville, before setting off again for Rucqueville, Esquay-sur-Seulles and Sommervieu. Other units headed west. The 1st Hampshire moved along the coast and captured Arromanches in the early evening. The South Wales Borderers advanced beyond Magny to discover the Vaux battery, unmanned in the aftermath of the terrible naval shelling. A few miles further north, the battery at Longues had, in spite of the night's bombing and since the dawn, been engaged in a fight to the finish with the big ships that seemed to be defying it. Finally, the combined firepower of the Ajax, the Arkansas, the Georges Leygues and the Montcalm definitively reduced it to silence during the evening, after a day of duelling. The 2nd Devon captured it the following morning, taking 150 prisoners.

Alert on the Atlantic Wall. This time it was not an exercise.

The 50ᵗʰ Infantry Division landing on Gold Beach. The LCI (Landing Craft Infantry) ramps, which had become slippery, provoked many a fall.

Many of the German troops were mere youngsters.

ALL MY NOTES ARE
AT THE BOTTOM OF THE SEA

HOWARD MARSHALL, BBC

I'M SITTING IN MY SOAKED-THROUGH CLOTHES WITH NO NOTES AT ALL; ALL MY NOTES ARE SODDEN - THEY'RE AT THE BOTTOM OF THE SEA. I'M JUST GOING TO TRY TO TELL YOU VERY BRIEFLY THE STORY OF WHAT OUR BOYS HAD TO DO ON THE BEACHES TODAY AS I SAW IT MYSELF.

THE LANDING CRAFT WERE LOWERED AND, AS THE LIGHT BROKE AND WE REALLY COULD SEE AROUND US, WE BEGAN TO BECOME AWARE OF THE FORMIDABLE CHARACTER OF THIS INVASION FLEET OF WHICH WE WERE A PART. WE COULD SEE AS WE WENT IN THAT OUR PARTICULAR PORTION OF THE BEACH WASN'T ALTOGETHER HEALTHY, BUT WE DROVE TOWARDS IT WITH OUR PLANES OVERHEAD GIVING US THE SORT OF COVER WE'D BEEN HOPING FOR, AND WHICH WE'D BEEN EXPECTING. AS WE DROVE IN WE COULD SEE SHELL BURSTS IN THE WATER ALONG THE BEACH, AND WE COULD SEE CRAFT IN A CERTAIN AMOUNT OF DIFFICULTY BECAUSE THE WIND WAS DRIVING THE SEA IN WITH LONG ROLLERS AND THE ENEMY HAD PREPARED ANTI-INVASION, ANTI-BARGE OBSTACLES STICKING OUT OF THE WATER – FORMIDABLE PRONGS, MANY OF THEM TIPPED WITH MINES, SO THAT AS YOUR LANDING CRAFT SWUNG AND SWAYED IN THE ROLLERS, AND THEY'RE NOT PARTICULARLY MANAGEABLE CRAFT, IT WOULD COME IN CONTACT WITH ONE OF THESE MINES AND BE SUNK. THAT WAS THE PROSPECT FACING US ON THIS VERY LOWERING AND DIFFICULT MORNING AS WE DROVE INTO THE BEACH.

AND SUDDENLY, AS WE TRIED TO GET BETWEEN TWO OF THESE TRIPARTITE DEFENCE SYSTEMS, OUR CRAFT SWUNG, WE TOUCHED A MINE, THERE WAS A VERY LOUD EXPLOSION, A THUNDERING SHUDDER OF THE WHOLE CRAFT, AND WATER BEGAN POURING IN. WELL, WE WERE SOME WAY OUT FROM THE BEACH AT THIS POINT. THE RAMP WAS LOWERED AT ONCE AND OUT OF THE BARGE DROVE THE BREN GUN CARRIER INTO ABOUT FIVE FEET OF WATER, WITH THE BARGE SETTLING HEAVILY IN THE MEANWHILE. WELL, THE BREN GUN CARRIER SOMEHOW MANAGED TO GET THROUGH IT, AND WE FOLLOWED WADING ASHORE. THAT WAS ONE QUITE TYPICAL INSTANCE OF HOW PEOPLE GOT ASHORE, AND WHEN THEY GOT ASHORE SEEMED TO BE IN PERFECTLY GOOD ORDER, BECAUSE THE TROOPS OUT OF THAT BARGE IMMEDIATELY ASSEMBLED AND WENT TO THEIR APPOINTED PLACES, AND THERE WAS NO SEMBLANCE OF ANY KIND OF CONFUSION. BUT THE SCENE ON THE BEACH, UNTIL ONE HAD SORTED IT OUT, WAS AT FIRST RATHER DEPRESSING BECAUSE WE DID SEE A GREAT MANY BARGES IN DIFFICULTIES WITH THESE ANTI-TANK SCREENS, AND WE NOTICED THAT A NUMBER OF THEM HAD STRUCK MINES, AS OURS HAD. BUT THEN WE BEGAN TO SEE THAT IN FACT THE PROPORTION THAT HAD GOT THROUGH WAS VERY MUCH GREATER, AND THAT THE TROOPS WERE MOVING ALL ALONG THE ROADS, AND THAT TANKS WERE OUT ALREADY AND GOING UP HILLS, THAT IN FACT WE DOMINATED THE SITUATION; AND THAT OUR MAIN ENEMY WAS THE WEATHER; THAT WE HAD OUR TROOPS AND TANKS ASHORE, AND THAT THE GERMANS WEREN'T REALLY PUTTING UP A GREAT DEAL OF RESISTANCE.

THE CANADIANS ON JUNO BEACH

The dangerous coastal reefs off Juno Beach made the approach to the beaches between Graye and Saint-Aubin particularly difficult. The German navy had gone as far as decreeing that an invasion in the sector was impossible. General Keller's powerful 3rd Canadian Infantry was going to have to prove them wrong. However, the navigation of the barges proved extraordinarily problematic. They had to wait until the tide was sufficiently high to get over the reefs without danger, but before it had covered the obstacles the Germans had installed all over the beaches, making them particularly dangerous. The operation, which was planned to the minute, did not go as hoped. Because of the heavy swell, the Canadians' arrival was held up for nearly half an hour and took place, somewhat chaotically and badly synchronised, around 8 o'clock. In one spot, the amphibious tanks arrived before the infantry; in another, they were sunk, or held up, and not where they should have been, any more than was the special equipment for the engineers, with the result that ill-equipped men were left to confront the German positions, that had been only relatively lightly damaged by the bombardments.

The beach was crowded with men and equipment.

Many of the landing craft became impaled on the stakes sticking out of the sand. Others were blown up by the mines or the shells fixed to the top of some of them. That was the fate of two of the five barges carrying a company of the Regina Rifles. The massacre was even worse when the empty barges tried to leave in reverse. Instead of liberating the edge of the beach, they made the congestion even worse. A third of the 300 assault barges used on the morning of 6th June were destroyed. Soldiers wallowed in the water, weighed down under their gear, and arrived exhausted on the beach to be met by bursts of machine gun fire and the explosions of mortar shells. The British of the N° 48 Royal Marine Commando, who landed east of Saint-Aubin in support of the Canadians, nearly met with disaster. On the beach, their losses were staggeringly high. They were still fighting in Langrune at nightfall, fighting to accomplish the link-up with Sword. By then, only 340 of the initial 630 men were still on their feet. A company of the Queen's Own Rifles lost half of their number in front of Bernières as they crossed the 100 yards to the protective sea-wall. At Courseulles, on Nan Green, "B" Company of the Regina Rifles captured the German positions with support from amphibious tanks, and without sustaining too many losses. Just to its right, however, "A" Company was less fortunate. All its supporting armour had sunk. They had to wait nearly two hours for a Centaur tank before getting the better of the 75-mm gun in a pillbox that was pinning them down. Between Courseulles and Graye, the "B" Company of the Winnipeg Rifles was sorely pressed. It had had the misfortune of landing directly opposite an enemy stronghold, the WN 31, equipped with anti-tank and machine guns.

Nevertheless, the Canadians fought with savage determination. These tough men were all volunteers, as the Ottawa government, enlightened by robust opposition to conscription (notably from the French-speakers) during the First World War, had renounced sending its

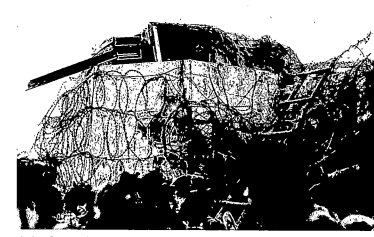

At La Cassine (Bernières), this fortified German machine gun emplacement wreaked havoc in the ranks of the Queen's Own Rifles.

Offloading bicycles on Nan White. They were supposed to make it possible for the infantry to reach Caen rapidly.

soldiers to fight outside the country without their consent. Their losses might have been appalling, but nothing was going to stop them.

New units landed on the cluttered beaches as best they could. The French Canadians of the Chaudière regiment set foot on Bernières beach half an hour after the first wave, under fire from the artillery and the mortars that had not yet been neutralised, so they had to make a clean sweep of the site before they could think of moving inland, towards Bény and Basly, with support from the tanks of the Fort Gary Horse. The 1st Canadian Scottish, who landed in a less heavily fortified sector at the western extremity of Juno Beach, advanced rapidly towards the village of Graye, which lay some small way back from the shore. They

left the Vaux castle sanatorium, which was occupied by a detachment of die-hard Russian gunners who held out until the next day, and made straight for Sainte-Croix. In Saint-Aubin and Courseulles, which were both formidably fortified, fierce fighting continued, often terminating with the use of grenades and hand-to-hand combat. Sometimes, it was only by using the special tanks that could launch the massive "flying dustbin" explosive charges that they managed to deal with the concrete ramparts. A few pockets of German resistance were still in action after the main body of the Canadian troops had begun driving inland towards Reviers, Sainte-Croix, Tailleville, Pierrepont, Fontaine-Henry, Anguerny... leaving around a thousand dead or wounded on the beaches.

Units of the 3rd Canadian Infantry Division landing at Bernières; the sea was already up to the sea wall.

A "family" reunion: locals from Bernières were amazed to meet the French-speaking Canadians of the Chaudière Regiment.

NORMANDY...
HOME FROM HOME

MARCEL OUIMET, *RADIO CANADA*

WE HAVE ONLY BEEN IN FRANCE FOR FIVE DAYS, BUT IT WOULD SEEM, ABOVE ALL FOR THE FRENCH-SPEAKING CANADIANS, THAT WE HAVE ALWAYS BEEN HERE. NORMANDY, THIS NORMANDY THAT ONE ALWAYS WANTS TO SEE AGAIN, JUST AS THE SONG SAYS. AFTER ALL, IT'S SORT OF HOME TO US, NOW THAT SOME OF OUR BOYS ARE SLEEPING THEIR LAST SLEEP UNDER THIS RICH SOIL THAT THEIR ANCESTORS LEFT TO GO AND FOUND A NEW FRANCE.

YES, WE FRENCH-SPEAKING CANADIANS HAVE HAD THE IMPRESSION THAT WE ARE RETURNING HOME. THESE LITTLE VILLAGES STILL BEDECKED WITH FLOWERS, AND PRETTY, IN SPITE OF THE BOMBARDMENT, THE SPIRES ON THE NORMAN CHURCHES – SEVERAL OF THEM WERE BUILT BY WILLIAM THE CONQUEROR – THE COUNTRYSIDE, THE GREENERY, THE PHYSICAL APPEARANCE OF THE INHABITANTS, THEIR ACCENT, THIS ACCENT THAT HAS LED THEM TO EXCLAIM: "BUT YOU'RE FAE'ROUND HERE!" TO SEVERAL OF OUR SOLDIERS. SO MANY ELEMENTS REMINISCENT OF OUR FRENCH REGIONS IN CANADA. THEY WERE ASTONISHED TO HEAR THE GUYS FROM QUEBEC SAY, "BUT I HAIL FROM TROIS PISTOLES," AND THEY LAUGHED EVEN HARDER WHEN THEY ASKED THEM IF THEY WOULD SOON BE IN PARIS, AND WERE ANSWERED IN TYPICAL NORMAN FASHION *"P'TÊT BEN QU'OUI"* ("MAYBE, WE'LL SEE..."). THE SOLDIERS THEMSELVES WERE DELIGHTED WITH THE ADVENTURE. "A RIGHT BONNY COUNTRY," AS THEY SAID, HAVING HARDLY SEEN ANYTHING OF FRANCE; A BIT LIKE THE ANSWERS GIVEN TO A FRENCH JOURNALIST TRAVELLING ACROSS THE COUNTRY BY A CANADIAN FARMER BEFORE THE GREAT WAR, UPON BEING ASKED WHAT HE THOUGHT OF HIS ANCESTORS' FATHERLAND: "FRANCE, SIR, IS A RIGHT GOOD PERSON."

THE SECOND BATTLE FOR FRANCE IS PERHAPS NOT YET WON, BUT WE CAN SAFELY SAY THAT OUR SOLDIERS HAVE WON THE HEARTS OF THE LIBERATED POPULATIONS, AND IT IS FINE AND FITTING THAT SOLDIERS FROM HOME CAN CONTRIBUTE TO GIVING THE NORMANS, THE FIRST FRENCHMEN TO BE LIBERATED IN FRANCE ITSELF, THE OPPORTUNITY, THE CHANCE, OF RECOVERING THEIR FATHERLAND AND THEIR NATIONAL SELF-ESTEEM.

THE GREEN BERETS ATTACK ON SWORD BEACH

The barges approached the assault zone on Sword Beach, between Lion-sur-Mer and the Orne estuary, assigned to General Rennie's British 3rd Infantry Division, with support from two commando brigades, the famous "*Green Berets*". One of them included Lord Lovat, commanding officer of the 1st Special Service (Commando) Brigade. The eccentric and heart-warming scene, of the sort that the British appreciate so much, had this noble Scottish lord flanked by his personal bagpiper, playing ancient and traditional airs on his pipes. They were to land to the skirl of "*Blue Bonnets*". Elsewhere, an officer was declaiming Shakespeare, reciting Henry V's famous harangue to his troops on the day before the battle of Agincourt. By a curious piece of historical irony, these men were going to have to capture Ouistreham, precisely at the spot where a monument commemorated the memory of a landing by the English ... valiantly repelled by the French in 1792.

The commandos launching the assault. In the foreground, the famous piper Bill Millin with his bagpipes. On his left, in the water, Lord Lovat, brigade commander.

The East Yorkshires grappling with a certain degree of chaos on Queen Red.

Leaving the powerfully fortified ends of the beach for the time being, the main body of troops attacked in the centre, in the Queen Beach sector, at Hermanville and Colleville. Here, as elsewhere, the most difficult moment was getting across the beach. The East Yorkshire regiment was given a rough time and lost 200 men. As the fighting continued, a lethal artillery barrage from inland hit the assailants. The Germans had no problems finding the range. The exact location of their targets was conveniently indicated by the barrage balloons floating just over the beach. They were intended to prevent diving attacks by enemy aviation. A futile precaution, because the *Luftwaffe* was anything but present in the Normandy sky on that decisive day. The sky was entirely free for the hordes of Allied fighter-bombers, hastily painted with wide black and white stripes to facilitate their identification. In spite of severe losses, of men and of armour, the British troops succeeded in breaking through. The place where they had landed was, auspiciously, called "*la Brèche*" (the Breach). There was still Ouistreham. A frontal attack would have resulted in a slaughter, as the Germans had developed a formidable defensive system. Thus, the "Green

Berets" of Commando N° 4 received orders to attack from behind. Amongst them were the 177 men of the French 1st Marine Battalion under Lieutenant Commander Philippe Kieffer. When they regrouped in the ruins of a holiday camp, west of the seaside resort, thirty of them were already missing, and the hardest part of their mission was yet to come: they had to approach the port by crossing right through Riva Bella, winding between ruins infested with isolated snipers. When they made it to the little station, the French soldiers left their British comrades, who headed for the lock and attacked the battery situated on the other side of the canal, and made for what was left of the former casino that the Germans had demolished in 1942 and transformed into a bunker. Although he was wounded, Kieffer led the assault himself, perched on the turret of a "DD" tank requisitioned nearby. A few well-placed shells put the 20-mm guns on top of the building out of action. Discouragement soon persuaded the remaining defenders to surrender.

Meanwhile, the 3rd Division's leading brigade had managed to drive into the interior and liberate the small towns of Hermanville and Colleville, while the

N° 41 Royal Marine Commando veered towards Lion-sur-Mer. As for the men of Lord Lovat's 1st Special Brigade, they headed for Bénouville and Ranville bridges to reinforce the paratroops there. Here, as elsewhere, the Atlantic Wall had crumbled before the Allied thrust. The follow-up was to be more fraught. The beach, which was becoming narrower as the tide rose, was crowded with men and machines. The narrowness of the small seaside towns' streets made it particularly difficult to move them out. None of this was to make their progress inland any easier, progress made all the more difficult by the presence of the 21st Panzer Division, whose forward units the British came up against between Colleville and the ridge at Périers-sur-le-Dan, where there were some robustly fortified positions. Although the "Morris" site only put up feeble resistance, the same could not be said of the solid defences harbouring the headquarters of the 736th Grenadier regiment, baptised "Hillman" by the British troops. The first assault, at the beginning of the afternoon, resulted

The inhabitants of Colleville cheering the long awaited arrival of the British.

in failure. After long hours of preparation, a second succeeded, and the position was captured little after 8 o'clock in the evening. It was judged prudent for the time being to ignore the radar station at Douvres, further west, which was equally well defended. It finally fell eleven days later, totally surrounded and isolated, after several hours of combat.

Infantry of the 3rd Division pinned down under German fire, sheltering as best they could behind a Churchill tank. For some of them, it was already too late.

On Queen White, various units belonging
to the 8th Brigade attempting to regroup.

THE INVASION HAS SUCCEEDED!

Now sure of its success, the SHAEF authorised the broadcast of a laconic official message on the BBC airwaves: *"Communiqué N°1: Under the command of General Eisenhower Allied naval forces, supported by strong air forces, began landing Allied armies this morning on the northern coast of France."* It was half past nine in the morning.

The world learns of the invasion

A few hours earlier, Radio Berlin had been the first to announce the news to the world. Their announcement was soon to be relayed by numerous Allied information agencies. The American press was thus able to reveal the sensational news in their editions dated 6th July. A cute journalistic exploit, greatly aided, naturally, by the differences across time zones. In New York people began praying in the street for the Allies' success. In Great Britain workers in their factories and housewives in their kitchens, stopped working to listen to the morning's bulletins. After a night of anguish, it was a radiant Churchill who arrived in the Commons at midday, to thunderous acclaim from both Labour and Conservative benches. In his pocket, he had a message from Stalin, who was reassured by the opening of the second front that he had been pleading for with the West to relieve the burden incumbent on the Red Army.

The world learning the great news.

The war was over for these Germans, waiting on the beach at Courseulles to be shipped to a prisoner-of-war camp in England or Canada.

In Germany, the news of the invasion, which was broadcast the same day, spread like wildfire. It came as a breath of fresh hope for prisoners of war and deportees alike. In Dachau, Edmond Michelet was informed by one of his comrades. Here, at last was the "*great news we have yearned for, for so many days and nights, for so many weeks, for so many months: that news the expectation of which has nourished our lives more than the food that has been used to starve us.*"

In France, the news of the invasion spread fast, too. Whereas emotion and hope welled up in the hearts of the majority, the reactions of the Vichy government were not in tune with them. The old Marshal Pétain advised prudence: "*Do not worsen our misfortune by actions that might bring tragic reprisals down on your heads.*" Laval was more direct: "*France has signed the armistice. This war is not ours; you must not participate in this combat.*" General de Gaulle proudly answered him a few hours later: "*The supreme battle has begun. Of course, it is the battle for France and it is France's battle! For the sons of France, wherever they may be, whoever they may be, their simple and sacred duty is to fight the enemy with every means at their disposal!*"

In Berchtesgaden, Hitler awoke at 10 o'clock in the morning. If we are to believe those who were with him,

he was in an excellent mood, convinced as he was that the glorious *Wehrmacht* would soon throw the assailants back into the sea, after which victory he could concentrate his forces on the Eastern front. At the beginning of the afternoon, he gave the necessary orders for several armoured divisions to be moved in the direction of Normandy, but he refused to allow the 15th Army to intervene, and abandon their station north of the Seine. The attack on Normandy might well be a feint, as his intelligence services believed to be the case, intended to weaken the Pas-de-Calais. The Führer, who was still bamboozled by Fortitude's tricks, reacted without vigour in these crucial moments and lost precious time... that he was never to make up.

The 21st Panzer, the only armoured unit stationed in Normandy, south west of Caen and less than 13 miles from the coast, had to wait until the beginning of the afternoon before launching its counter-offensive against the beachhead. Too late, the majority of the tanks were to run into the British. Only one battalion managed to infiltrate the lines and reach Luc-sur-Mer at the end of the day, taking advantage of the corridor left open between the Sword and Juno sectors. It was isolated, afraid of becoming surrounded, and retreated rapidly without having been able to exploit the situation.

Daily Herald

STOP PRESS — PANZERS MOVE UP

WEDNESDAY, JUNE 7, 1944 — ONE PENNY — No. 8827

Invasion Army Ashore On Broad Front In France

ALLIES SEVERAL MILES INLAND

Airtroops Seize Important Bridges: Tanks Fight Way Into Defences

SHAEF COMMUNIQUE AT MIDNIGHT:—

WEATHER HELD IT UP 24 HOURS

2,000 Tons In First

STRAITS — Rain—But Sea Was Smooth

NEW INVASION FLEET OFF LE HAVRE—NAZIS

F.D.R. Confers With Service Chiefs

Stars And Stripes On Gone-West Wall

TOMMIES WENT IN WI'

Hospitals By Air

Le Matin

LE MIEUX INFORMÉ DES JOURNAUX FRANÇAIS

01ᵉ ANNÉE — N° 21.811 — PARIS — MERCREDI 7 JUIN 1944 — 5ᶠ

LA FRANCE REDEVIENT UN CHAMP DE BATAILLE

LES ANGLO-AMÉRICAINS ONT DÉBARQUÉ HIER MATIN ENTRE CHERBOURG ET L'EMBOUCHURE DE LA SEINE

Des combats acharnés se déroulent sur la côte, aux points les plus proches de Caen, centre de gravité des opérations

L'ennemi reconnaît qu'il a perdu 25.000 hommes au cours de cette première journée d'opération

EN FIN DE SOIRÉE, L'ENVAHISSEUR A ÉTÉ CONTRAINT D'ÉVACUER PLUSIEURS DE SES TÊTES DE PONT

PLUSIEURS DIVISIONS AÉROPORTÉES OU PARACHUTÉES ONT ÉTÉ CAPTURÉES

...e de force ...mencée

M. Philippe Henriot, à Berlin rend hommage à la Waffen SS

Le maréchal Pétain exhor... solennellement les Français au calme et à la discipline

« N'aggravez pas nos malheurs par des actes qui entraîneraient le pays au désastre »

« La France a signé l'armistice elle doit faire honneur à sa signature » proclame le président Laval

---

EXTRA!

Los Angeles Times

9 A.M. FINAL — TUESDAY MORNING, JUNE 6, 1944 — DAILY, FIVE CENTS

INVASION!

4000 S... 11,000 at Fre...

SUPREME EXPEDITI... Allied force...

LAST MINUTE INVASION BULL...

VÖLKISCHER BEOBACHTER

Münchener Ausgabe — 159. Ausg. 57. Jahrg. Einzelpreis 15 Rpf., 20 Rpf.

Kampfblatt der nationalsozialistischen Bewegung Großdeutschlands

München, Mittwoch, 7. Juni 1944

Invasion setzte zwischen Cherbourg und Le Havre auf Moskaus Befehl ein

So begann die Schlacht im Westen

Der mit aller Energie sofort aufgenommene Kampf unserer Wehrmacht gegen die Aggressoren ist in vollem Gange

Die Sowjetoffensive am Kanal

Starke Teile der Luftlandedivisionen vernichtet

Um Leben und Freiheit Europas

Es geht um die Entscheidung

Der Schauplatz der Invasion

Friendly contact between the population in Bernières and the Canadians.

An assessment of a historic day

The front line was extending imperceptibly inland away from the shoreline, which was still smoking from the morning's fighting. In the British sector, near Bernières, Courseulles and Ouistreham, there was an extraordinarily intense activity on the beaches as the afternoon drew to a close. The LCI troops carriers could by now come into the shore in safety. Long lines of soldiers descended the ramps, one on each side of their bows, to wade through the last few yards of water, bicycles over their shoulders. The shore was littered with masses of equipment. Newly landed half-tracks, field guns, tanks and trucks lay beside or wound their way between the wreckage testifying to the bitterness of the fighting at dawn. Here and there, a few inhabitants conversed as best they could with the Allied soldiers over a few good bottles, set aside for this great occasion a long time previously. The children swarmed around these friendly, strapping fellows whose pockets were just stuffed with sweets and chocolate. During the battle, the civilians had

spent abominable hours at the bottom of trenches they had dug in their gardens. When calm returned, the incredible array of their liberators' power was displayed before their disbelieving eyes. There were hundreds of German prisoners sitting under the sea-walls and at the base of the dunes, glassy eyed and awaiting their turn to embark on the transport ships that were to take them to England. For them, the war was over. It had just begun for many others. On 6th June 1944 at midnight over 150,000 Allied soldiers, including 23,000 paratroops, and 20,000 vehicles of all shapes and sizes were already on Norman soil. Less than 10,000 men (killed, wounded or captured) had been lost, well below the planning department's predictions: they had expected 25,000 men to be lost. With the exception of Omaha beach, where the American vanguard were still practically with their backs to the sea, and Colonel Rudder's rangers who were surrounded on the Pointe du Hoc, all the other bridgeheads already extended half a dozen miles into the interior.

An American paratrooper, wounded... but happy to be back with his comrades after long hours of isolation in the Normandy countryside.

In Amfreville, a reunion between the Frenchmen in N° 4 Commando and their compatriots.

Off Utah beach, the 4th Division had linked up with the paratroops of the 101st in Pouppeville. The fate of the men of the 82nd Airborne, who had been dropped further west, was more worrying; most of them, scattered in little groups in the middle of German territory, were engaged in confused skirmishing. The British 50th Division, which had landed on Gold beach, reached the gates of Bayeux in the small hours of the following morning and captured it without firing a shot. The Canadians had covered a record 7 miles or so, and had reached as far as Villons-les-Buissons, but had not managed to capture their main objective, the Carpiquet aerodrome, near Caen. Lovat's 1st Special Brigade reached the bridges at Bénouville and Ranville at the beginning of the afternoon, where they linked up with the 6th Airborne. Towards 9 o'clock in the evening, the latter was to receive fresh reinforcements with the arrival of 250 gliders, including

thirty-odd big Hamilcar gliders carrying guns and light tanks. Meanwhile, the British 3rd Division had set out in the direction of Caen, with orders to capture it if possible, but its progress had been hampered by the build-up of bottle-necks of equipment on the coast, and by doughty pockets of German resistance. The dithering of a few commanders, who were more concerned with occupying the territory they had won than striking forward, did the rest. By the time the head of the column reached the outskirts of Caen, the Germans had had enough time to organise a solid barrage of tanks and infantry there. The British, stymied at the Lebisey woods, were not to capture Caen that evening. They were to have to wait a whole month before gaining that particular prize. All in all, the landings had been a success, but the game was still anyone's. The Battle of Normandy had begun. It was to last nearly three long months.

The 21st Panzer, the only German armoured division near the invasion sector, was unable to repel the Allies.

The British 27th Armoured Brigade preparing to land on Sword on barges brimming over with vehicles.

In Ver-sur-Mer, soldiers of the 50th Division killed during the invasion were buried in a temporary cemetery.

NORMAN TOWNS CRUSHED BY BOMBS

Throughout the day on 6th June, the Allied aviation filled the Normandy sky. Dawn brought the Americans, who began their relay of the British. Stations, crossroads and bridges were attacked without respite, more or less successfully, as the weather conditions were far from ideal. In Caen, the offensives against the bridges over the Orne were miserable failures. At half past one in the afternoon whole strings of bombs were dropped off target... but on the town centre, destroying it all the way from the river to the Castle and killing nearly 500 people. This was but the first of many of the day's tragedies for the Norman population. Later, at 7 o'clock in the evening, hundreds of B-17 Flying Fortresses and B-24 Liberators took off ponderously from their bases in the south of England. These aircraft of the 8th US Air Force were soon flying over the Channel in tight formation. There were 750 in all, each of them carrying several tonnes of bombs.

The ruins of the Saint-Jacques church in Lisieux.

In the early evening light, these big four-engined planes were to accomplish their last, but without doubt the most terrible mission on that fated day. Their business was destroying a dozen Norman towns lying on the arc running from Pont-l'Évêque through to Coutances. By reducing them to ruins, it was the Allies' intention to shatter the communications networks they were the main hubs of, and to paralyse - or at least considerably slow down - the arrival of German reinforcements at the bridgehead. The stakes were worth the penalty in the opinion of the military commanders. The destruction of the Norman towns had thus been programmed, however high a price it seemed to have to pay. It was, at this precise instant, only a few minutes away. No-one was ignorant of the amount of carnage that these massive bombardments would create. The American Generals, who were more concerned about the fate of civilian populations than were their British counterparts, made it known that the bombing of French cities without military installations was a "*detestable thing*". In the end, they had to go with the general movement, but not before obtaining a decision whereby tracts were to be dropped in large numbers at dawn on 6th June, warning citizens and encouraging them to leave the cities as early as possible. Unfortunately, most of them were swept far from their targets, having been dropped from too great a height. Those rare individuals who did find one were for the most part incredulous and did not take the warning seriously. The time was just after 8 o'clock in the evening. The bombers were divided into several groups and were over their targets. The bomb holds

Caen burning after a bombardment by Bomber Command that lasted three-quarters of an hour.

were opened. The first clusters of bombs were simultaneously dropped on Pont-l'Évêque, Lisieux, Vire, Condé-sur-Noireau, Flers, Coutances, Saint-Lô...

Many of those who heard the muffled throbbing hum of the bombers' engines approaching came out onto their doorsteps to admire these great white planes reflecting the pale rays of the setting sun. Many of them interrupted their meals to take in the impressive spectacle. They would never finish that meal. They unwarily watched death drawing near. Then came the cataclysm! Brutal and unforeseen. The scene was brief but terrible. There was an enormous crashing roar of bombs exploding. The ground and the walls were shaking. Houses crumbled in clouds of dust. The drama only lasted a few seconds, and yet whole areas of towns were pulverised. The first wave passed on, but the following minutes

brought more, putting the finishing touches to the massacre. Hundreds of men, women and children were never to see the end of that historic day; it began with euphoria and finished with tragedy. The same horrific scenes were everywhere: screaming, weeping, haggard victims, covered in dust and blood, running in all directions through the rubble. When the first moments of stupefaction had passed, the rescue operation got under way as best it could. The men of the civil defence came with stretchers and did their best to release those who were trapped. Fires broke out here and there; but the firemen were helpless as their equipment had, as often as not, been destroyed. The bombers flew back to England, leaving death and desolation behind them. In Stanmore, Air Marshal Mallory's HQ, the strategists were dissatisfied with the results.

Saint-Lô was razed by the Allied aviation during the night of 6th-7th June.

The shop Monoprix on fire following the first attack on Caen at half past one in the afternoon.

Caen: the Rue de Geole on the morning of 7th June.

The first reports showed that the bombardment's objectives had only been partially achieved. Some squadrons had not been able to identify their targets, and had returned home with a full load of bombs. Falaise escaped disaster in this way, at least temporarily, as did Thury-Harcourt. Flers, which had been mistaken for Argentan, was flattened in its stead. The terrible decision was soon taken: the bombardment must recommence. Vire, Condé-sur-Noireau, Lisieux, Argentan, Saint-Lô and Coutances were all on the diabolical list, with a new addition, Caen, which the Allies had not succeeded in capturing on D-Day itself as they had planned. Night fell, and it was the RAF who shouldered the chore, as their pilots were used to nocturnal missions. Shortly after midnight, a thousand Lancaster and Halifax bombers were flying towards the martyred towns, where the rescue squads were still busy in the rubble. Brutally, flares lit up the ruins with

their intense brightness, creating a lugubrious shadow-play on the broken walls. The British bombers circled methodically over their prey in a hellish carousel that in some cases lasted several tens of minutes. In Caen, a constant stream of bombs fell between half past two and three o'clock in the morning. Gigantic fires flared up all over town. Windows burst and walls crumbled in a horrendous din. The flames from the fires were visible for miles around. The towns all had a fire-red halo. It seemed as if the sky itself had caught fire.

Fortunately, a sizeable proportion of the population had run away to hide in the surrounding areas; another massacre was thus avoided, except in Caen, where there were around 200 supplementary victims added to the afternoon's list, and particularly in Lisieux. In Saint Theresa's town, the evening attack had only caused minor damage, except near the railway station.

Many of Caen's inhabitants left town on the afternoon of 6th June, fleeing from the bombardments. Here, the Rue de l'Arquette.

Most of the Lexoviens (inhabitants of Lisieux) who believed that the risk was over, no longer thought it necessary to leave, so they were at home when the bombers returned at half past one in the morning and obliterated the centre of town. Nearly 700 of them were to perish during that tragic night of 6th-7th June, crushed under their fallen houses and often burnt alive. When dawn rose on 7th June, part of the towns of Lower Normandy had been scrubbed off the map: Caen, Lisieux, Coutances, Saint-Lô, Argentan, Condé-sur-Noireau... had all been transformed into a revolting magma of stone, cinder and ash.

In total, the bombardment cost the lives of 3,000 men, women and children, equivalent to the number of Allied soldiers killed on the beaches the previous morning.

Place des Petites Boucheries, heading west.

FIGHTING IN NORMANDY

"*There is a very big difference between a given battle or campaign plan and the results of the operation. The battle for the bridgehead involved incessant and savage fighting during which, with the exception of the capture of Cherbourg, territorial gains were rather small. Nevertheless, it was there that the spectacular liberation of France and Belgium was begun.*"

Dwight D. Eisenhower, Commander-in-Chief of operation Overlord.

THE BATTLE FOR THE BRIDGEHEAD (7th-18th JUNE)

ON 6th June 1944, the Allies succeeded in establi-shing a toe-hold on the Normandy coast, but their positions were precarious and the adversary, who had been taken by surprise, was not to be long in reacting. The battle for the consolidation and the extension of the bridgehead began at that moment. The next ten days were to prove decisive. Everyone was aware of that. For the Anglo-Americans, it was a case of landing fresh troops as quickly as possible, while preventing or hindering the arrival of enemy reinforcements on the Norman coast for as long as possible.

Under his command, Von Rundstedt had 27 avai-lable divisions, 4 of them armoured, within a radius of 200 miles around the landing zone, in addition to those already engaged in the fighting. In theory, it would only take a few days to get them to the front, where the Germans would then have an enormous numerical advantage. The Allies' would *a priori* require more time to gather their forces. They would be reduced to fighting one against two, and in those conditions ran the risk of being brutally thrown back into the sea.

The incredible deployment of Allied forces on the Normandy beachhead.

The German convoys were prey to the terrible Allied fighter-bombers.

Hell on the roads for the German reinforcements

Most fortunately, this scenario was not destiny's choice. The *Wehrmacht* High Command, which had still not tumbled to the fact that operation Fortitude was a hoax, obstinately refused to thin out their defences on the coasts of Upper Normandy and Picardy, however close they were. It preferred the idea of moving the units stationed in Brittany, in southern France, and sometimes from even further afield.

Before they made it to Normandy, these units were to go through a veritable ordeal under the combined and devastatingly efficient operations of the Allied tactical aviation and the Resistance. The destruction of the rail network by the spring bombardments and the sabotage undertaken from the night of 5th June onwards, constrained the Germans to use the roads, where they were to be sitting ducks for the fighter-bombers, the famous "*Jabos*" (*Jagdbombe*) that were to haunt many a memory. Spitfires, Thunderbolts and Lightnings wheeled overhead, filling the sky with their incessant hum like a swarm of hornets, mercilessly striking the convoys whose makeshift camouflage of branches hid them rather inadequately. The terrible Typhoons, armed with four 20-mm cannons and rocket launchers, were the most feared of all. The trees felled by the partisans and lying across the road halted the convoys and made them easy game. Bodies and the burnt-out shells of vehicles began clogging up the verges of the routes leading to Lower Normandy. To avoid being massacred, the Germans were obliged forthwith to manoeuvre only under cover of night; but the hours of darkness were favourable to the daring strikes organised by members of the Resistance, responsible for hindering further the arrival of reinforcements.

The 275th Infantry Division took a week to cover the 150 miles between Lorient and Saint-Lô, where they arrived in dribs and drabs, as a number of them had had to come all the way from Pontorson on foot. The *Panzer Lehr*, which came from Chartres, had already lost part of its equipment and tanks when it took up position to the west of Caen. It took the 2nd Panzer SS, *Das Reich*, nearly three weeks to reach Normandie from Toulouse region.

True, it had received the order to clean up pockets of the Resistance and other underground movements en route. We know the manner in which it obeyed those orders, leaving death and desolation in its wake: a hundred inhabitants of Tulle hanged from street lamps; and the little village of Oradour-sur-Glane annihilated along with its population. The 9th and 10th *Panzerdivisions* SS reached Alsace in four days from the Eastern front, but it subsequently took them two weeks to cross French territory to the Western front – much too late to participate in the - oft planned but ever postponed - massive German armoured counter-offensive.

The German vehicles used camouflage to blend in with their surroundings. The soldier on the mudguard is keeping an eye out for planes.

The growing power of the Allies

Meanwhile, the Allies' forces were swelling daily, to the tune of 30,000 men, 7,000 vehicles and 30,000 tonnes of supplies on average. Neither the *Luftwaffe*, nor the *Kriegsmarine* managed to dam the colossal influx of the armies of freedom. The few dozen submarines sent to the Channel by Admiral Doenitz spent more time defending themselves than attacking. As for the black-crossed planes, and in spite of receiving reinforcements, very few seemed eager to run the risk of challenging the Allied fighters, to the great displeasure of the troops on the ground, who joked, not without some bitterness: "*If you see a white plane in the sky, it's American; a black one, it's British; when you don't see anything, it's the Luftwaffe!*"

Between 6th and 30th June, the German aviation was to notch up a little over 10,000 sorties, compared to 140,000 by the Allies. The *Luftwaffe*, which was more or less absent by day, was very much more active at night, notably along the beaches, and sometimes did quite serious damage to the Allies or the civilian populations. For example, on 2nd July, a mine attached to a parachute fell on a villa in Lion-sur-Mer, killing fifteen people in one blow. Off the Normandy coast, the activity was intense. The warships were still supporting the ground troops with their powerful guns bombarding the enemy positions, subjecting them to extraordinarily precise and very heavy shelling as far as 12 miles inland.

Colonel van der Heydte's storm-troopers put up fierce resistance around Carentan.

The 12th Panzer SS Hitlerjugend en route for Caen.

Ships of all sizes began an incredible ballet, sheltered behind the "Gooseberries", lines of sunken ships that had been scuttled on site from the morning of 7th June onwards off all five beaches. The imposing LSTs beached their bows on the beaches, and disgorged tanks and trucks from their bellies. At sea, big freighters loaded equipment onto metallic "Rhinos" that carried it to the shore. The amphibious DUCKW trucks roared out of the water in showers of foam and spray and accelerated away from the beaches towards the front lines with their loads of ammunition. The little ports of Courseulles and Port-en-Bessin were put to work with a will. Off Arromanches and Saint-Laurent, the British and the Americans began a peaceful competition to see who would be the first to complete the construction of their artificial harbour. In Port-en-Bessin and in Sainte-Honorine-des-Pertes, men busied themselves with the job of setting up the PLUTO system, making it possible to transfer fuel from tankers at anchor in the Channel directly to fuel dumps built on land, by a system of flexible pipe-lines. Without losing a moment, teams began preparing airstrips on the Norman soil. The first, which were operational on 7th June, in Pouppeville (Sainte-Marie-du-Mont), Saint-Laurent-sur-Mer, and Asnelles, were emergency aerodromes, consecrated to aircraft in difficulty and the evacuation of the seriously wounded back to England. More followed, designed to accommodate squadrons of fighter-bombers. The engineers had an impressive array of equipment at their disposal, to the surprise of the locals. Hedges were razed and land was levelled using bulldozers and scrappers, before being covered with steel matting or metal grates. In all, fifty aerodromes or so were built during July and August 1944, most of them in the Bessin and the Cotentin. They were to make it possible for the Allied tactical air forces to greatly increase their offensive capacity and shoulder the capital role they played in the struggle for Normandy.

Construction of a British airfield. A Typhoon is taking off in the background.

Mechanics reloading the machine-guns on a P-47 Thunderbolt belonging to the 50th Fighter Group.

In less then ten days, the Allies had won the battle for the bridgehead. On 18th June, 600,000 men had been landed, along with 100,000 vehicles. Their power had grown faster than the Germans', and they had succeeded in rapidly linking the different assault zones.

The gap left open between Sword and Juno beaches was closed on 7th June. Towards midday on the 8th, a column came to the rescue of the Rangers on the Pointe du Hoc. High time too, as Colonel Rudder only had 90 able bodied men left in his contingent: eighty of their comrades had fallen on that tiny corner of Norman soil. That same day, contact was established between the British 50th Infantry Division and the GIs who had landed at Omaha. After the thrashing they had taken on the beaches on the morning of the 6th, these GIs were staging a spectacular recovery. The German soldiers, who were exhausted and deprived of supplies, had fallen to pieces after their doughty

resistance on D-Day itself. Their collapse left a gaping hole, which their adversaries piled into, motivated by the arrival of fresh divisions. The Americans, preceded by terrifying artillery barrages, smashed everything in their way and penetrated deep into the Bessin. In a few days, their bludgeoning had brought them as far as Balleroy, then Caumont-l'Éventé; twenty-odd miles inland. General Marcks, commander of the 84th Army Corps, was killed on 12th June by an Allied aircraft as he was arriving in the sector with the intention of reorganising its defence. Meanwhile, another westward thrust was under way towards the Cotentin. The little town of Isigny, famous for its dairy products, was captured on 9th June, after having been almost totally annihilated by violent naval shelling that cost the lives of some forty inhabitants. On the other side of the Baie des Veys, the men of the 101st Airborne were crossing the marshes around the river Douve to

In the ruins of Isigny.

attack Carentan, which they captured after fierce fighting on 12th June, despite the resistance put up by Colonel van der Heydte's storm troops. The next day, they energetically repelled the powerful counter-offensive mounted by the 17th *S Panzergrenadierdivision*, and they captured the dangerous and hitherto unconquered "wedge" between the Utah and Omaha sectors. The Allies now controlled an uninterrupted bridge head about sixty miles long, stretching from Quinéville in the west, to the Dives in the east.

Bayeux, leisure time for the British troops.

12ᵗʰ June 1944: Carentan in American hands.

The two countenances of the war

The British entered Bayeux without difficulty on 7ᵗʰ June in the morning, making it the first French town to be liberated by the Allies. From then on, an unusual fervour gripped the normally more reserved and austere bishopric. French tricolours fluttered beside Union Jacks and Stars and Stripes. The streets were full of soldiers, from busy, preoccupied officers to tipsy soldiers strolling arm in arm with smiling lasses. There were also some

French officers, including Lieutenant Maurice Schumann, the spokesman of the Free French, well known to all those who had been in the habit of listening to the BBC, who had landed at Courseulles on 6th June. He addressed the people of Bayeux every day, giving them the latest news, perched on the roof of a van draped in the colours of France and the Allies. The war correspondents from all the Allied countries set up their bases in Bayeux.

Cow and soldier.

Within the Allied armies, the Civil Affairs section was responsible for dealing with the problems of the liberated populations.

Unflagging conversation and debate, interspersed with laughter and the joyous chink of glasses and bottles, prevailed in the bistros and restaurants, which were never empty. Good wine and champagne that had miraculously reappeared accompanied feasting that was all the richer for the fact that the Bessin was no longer sending its meat and butter to the rest of France. Many drew the somewhat hasty conclusion, forgetting that this was an unusual occasion, that the Normans must have had a comfortable time of it under the occupation.

Churchill himself came to visit the bridgehead on 12th June: "*The weather was marvellous. We were progressing through our Norman domain, which was still cramped, but remarkably fertile, delighted with the prosperity of the countryside. The fields were full of superb russet and white cows, warming themselves or majestically parading in the sun. The inhabitants, who seemed cheerful and well fed, welcomed us with enthusiasm.*"

The war in Normandy in that summer of 1944 really did have two distinct aspects. On one side, the liberated, smi-

Father Prod'homme, the Vaux-sur-Seulles parish priest, giving RAF servicemen lessons in French pronunciation.

ling regions; on the other, the ugly spectre of war rearing up in a paroxysm of violence. That of young men killing each other in the cornfields and pastures. That of villages destroyed and cowering civilians caught in the crossfire. That of the seventy or eighty Resistance fighters summarily executed by the Gestapo at dawn on 6th June in the sordid back yards of the prison in Caen.

The airmen and the ground crews were more sedentary than their comrades in the army, and got involved with the locals.

The Normans
and their Liberators

THE ARTIFICIAL HARBOURS

The first elements of the artificial harbours arrived on the Normandy coast on the day immediately after D-Day. They were drawn by tugs to the two chosen sites. Mulberry "A" was to be built off Vierville/Saint-Laurent in the American sector, and Mulberry "B" off Arromanches in the British sector. Then an incredible game of full-scale, aquatic Meccano began for the teams commanded by Rear Admiral Tennant.

The artificial harbour at Omaha Beach. The liaison between the "Spud" pierhead on stilts and dry land was by floating causeway.

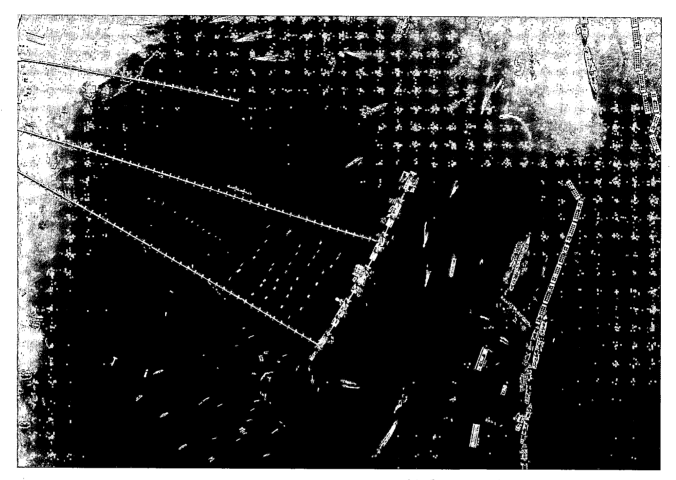

A bird's eye view of the artificial harbour in Arromanches.

A gigantic "aquatic Meccano" set

Each of the two harbours was protected from the swell by a breakwater, running parallel to the shore, consisting partly of the Gooseberries that were already in place, and completed by the Phoenixes. These massive hollow reinforced concrete caissons were towed across the Channel before being filled with water, once on site, in order to settle them on the seabed. The largest units weighed 6,000 tonnes, were 60 yards in length, 17 wide, and were as tall as a five storey building. Others, which were installed perpendicular to the shore, formed lateral breakwaters. Altogether, the protected area thus created was as capacious as Dover port, with a surface area of about 1,250 acres. Ships could enter and leave by one of several openings. The outer floating breakwater was moo-

red farther out to sea. It was made of a series of x cross-sectioned metal buoys, the Bombardons, each one measuring about 60 yards, filled with ballast in their lower sections and firmly anchored. The off-loading of the ships and the transfer of freight to the shore was unquestionably the most complex problem to solve, because of the tide. But British ingenuity was never at a loss as to how to cope.

The engineers developed pontoons consisting of an assembly of large metal platforms capable of sliding up and down thirty-yard high steel pillars, depending on the tide. Thence, transit to dry land was made by floating causeways each several hundred yards long, consisting of series of steel plates that were linked to create flexible steel roadways (Whales) that floated on

Fixing a causeway of floating pontoons to the landing quay.
The two floats were used to adjust its level.

A team of American engineers preparing the access ramp to the beach.

hollow concrete caissons, nick-named "Beetles" after their shape. Thanks to their flexibility, they rose and fell with the rhythm of the tides, thus avoiding any interruption in the off-loading operations. The whole scheme was completed on land by the organisation of depots, parks, and storage areas, whereas the existing roads were widened and new ones opened across fields to facilitate the rapid deployment of the vast fleet of lorries, guns, tanks, ammunition and men headed for the front. Less than ten days after the landings, and although the constructions were far from complete, the first landing installations were operational.

The Gooseberry off Utah Beach, a breakwater consisting of a line of scuttled ships.

High winds blew in the Channel from 19th – 21st June

The tempest (19th - 21st June)

19th June was to be a bad day for the Allies. That day, a North Easterly near gale blew up in the Channel, weather that had not been recorded in that season for over three quarters of a century. It was to last three days, and caused wide ranging damage.

At sea, a convoy of floating pontoons was submerged along with some of the old tugs that were towing them to Normandy. The two artificial harbours, which had not yet been completed and were not designed to withstand this kind of punishment, were even more severely damaged. The one off

Saint-Laurent was the more badly hit. Nearly half the Phoenixes were wrecked, having been crashed into by drifting Bombardons. The floating causeways and quays were almost completely wiped out. The Mulberry "B" at Arromanches fared better, but needed major repairs even so. The British – slightly mockingly – emphasised the fact that the Americans had ignored their advice and left too many openings in the artificial breakwater, thus weakening it.

When the wind dropped, the coast was a spectacle of desolation. Nearly 800 boats of all types: LCAs,

MSTs and even a destroyer, HMS Fury, (which had previously been damaged by a mine) were scattered along the beaches, inextricably entwined with the debris of the floating jetties and other wrecks. This was a major blow, as the damage was five times greater than that done by the Germans since 6th June. During the tempest and the days that followed, circulation dropped from 24,000 tonnes to 4,500 tonnes per day, temporarily depriving the troops of supplies and reinforcements, thus slowing down their progress.

In the face of the scale of the disaster, the Americans decided not to repair their artificial harbour. The elements that were still intact were salvaged and used to mend the British one. Nevertheless, they consolidated the Gooseberry, and reinitiated the earlier technique of landing directly on the beaches. The method was less sophisticated, but no less efficient: the tonnage landed every day at Omaha was distinctly higher than that brought in over the Mulberry at Arromanches!

A metal "Rhinoferry"

Consequently, it is probably an exaggeration to suggest that the artificial harbour at Arromanches was the cornerstone of the invasion's success; but it will go down in history as a brilliant technical achievement.

The effects of the stormy weather on the artificial harbour at Omaha Beach.

BAYEUX 14th JUNE "IT'S DE GAULLE!"

On 14th June 1944, the destroyer "*La Combattante*" of the Free French Navy, steamed into the Normandy coast. De Gaulle was on board, accompanied by a dozen of his closest collaborators, such as the Generals Béthouard and Koenig, Admiral Thierry d'Argenlieu, Gaston Palewski, Hettier de Boislambert....

The General was worried. He was aware of the decisive importance of this visit to the Normandy bridgehead. It's goal was nothing less than the on-site imposition of the authority of the Provisional Government of the French Republic, which he had established a few days previously. How were the Anglo-Americans going to react? President Roosevelt, who let it be understood that he considered de Gaulle to be an "*apprentice dictator*", did not credit him with any substance as a representative, and refused to entrust him with France's destiny until the population had been consulted. In the meantime, he had decided to establish an Allied military government of the occupied territories (AMGOT), following the previous year's Italian example. For de Gaulle – and he did not omit to say so openly and clearly – that solution was perfectly unacceptable, as was the circulation of the money printed in the United States, albeit bearing a little French flag... but dollar-green. The political imbroglio was at its height, and the fate of the country depended largely on the outcome of this 14th June.

The General and his close colleagues set foot on French soil on the beach between Courseulles and Graye.

On French soil at last! The General and his friends set foot on home ground - for the first time in almost exactly four years - early in the afternoon on the beach between Courseulles and Graye. Whereas a part of his entourage headed straight for Bayeux, de Gaulle lit a cigarette and climbed aboard a jeep sporting the tricolour, and left for the castle in Creully where Montgomery was waiting for him.

After the interview, the General headed for Bayeux. The moment of truth, of his meeting with the French population, was approaching. For four years, he had fretted about the feeling the population might have about him. Perhaps he didn't realise it, but Normandy had demonstrated strong Gaullist sentiments very early on. The reports of the Vichy authorities, from as early as 1940, bear witness to the fact. Thanks to the BBC, everyone knew de Gaulle's voice, but many did not know his face, in spite of the postcards portraying him distributed by the Resistance. A short distance from Bayeux, the General passed two gendarmes and hailed them. They impeccably saluted this unknown officer. *"My friends, I am General de Gaulle..."* The bicycles fell on the ground. *"Would you be so kind as to turn back and tell people there that I am coming, so that I don't bump into anyone unexpectedly."*

General Montgomery receiving de Gaulle at Creully Castle.

The triumphant visit through the streets of Bayeux.

But in Bayeux, everything was ready. Guillaume Mercader, leader of the local Resistance, had been told of the impending visit by Boislambert, and had taken appropriate action. The population had been thoroughly informed by a car with loudspeakers driven through the town.

De Gaulle entered Bayeux at around half past three in the afternoon, to the sound of shouting: "*It's de Gaulle! There's de Gaulle! De Gaulle's here!*" Shopkeepers shut up their stores to join the growing crowd cheering the General and his companions. Many joined the cortege as it moved forward, preceded by laughing children, along streets decorated in the national colours. Even if he didn't show it, de Gaulle was troubled: "*A sort of stupor had seized the inhabitants, who burst out cheering or broke down in tears. Thus shall we all together, overwhelmed and brotherly, feeling the joy, the national pride and hope, arise from the pit of the abyss.*" The visit to the offices of the local administration, the *sous-préfecture*, where the important figures were foregathered, was brief. De Gaulle asked the *sous-préfet* Rochat some questions.

The General speaking. "We are all moved to be reunited in one of the first French towns to be liberated..."

The latter had prudently removed the photograph of Pétain which had hitherto adorned his desk. Unfortunately, he had forgotten the portrait of the Marshal hanging on the wall of the main reception room. Boislambert, who was purple with fury, tore it down, hook and plaster included, with an emphatic gesture. Once the incident was over, the group took their leave and headed for the Castle quadrangle, where the General was to make a short speech to the very sizeable crowd that had gathered there. A platform had been hastily put together under the century-old lime trees and a microphone was unceremoniously wired up to a lorry's battery. When de Gaulle started speaking, a ray of sunshine broke through the Normandy clouds, shone through the leaves and symbolically lit his silhouette in a halo of light.

After a vibrant rendition of the *Marseillaise*, the French National Anthem, de Gaulle and his friends extracted themselves from the crowd, not without some difficulty, and continued their journey through the liberated Bessin. They reached the little town of Isigny to find the mourning inhabitants waiting for them in the ruins. The General pronounced a few comforting words, from the base of what had once been a lamppost. The atmosphere was more sombre and more poignant here than it had been in Bayeux. The afternoon drew on and the small convoy set off along the coast for Courseulles. *"In every village,"* said Boislambert, *"the General insisted that we stop and he said* a few heartfelt words to those inhabitants, who welcomed us with enthusiasm and confidence. 'Is that really de Gaulle?' as one friendly old fellow asked me, as a young woman was exclaiming 'It's him! It's really him!' Everyone wanted to cheer him, see him, touch him. As an old Norman myself, I was astonished to see this almost southern display of emotion. Just before Grandcamp, in front of us in the road, there was a priest on his horse. We stopped. I went to shake the hand of the reverend fellow and told him the General wanted to speak to him. 'Shit, is that really him?' 'Ah, yes, Father, come and speak to him.'"

When they got back to La Combattante, after a full and rewarding day, de Gaulle looked very satisfied: "We have proved it... The French people has shown who they trust to shoulder the duty of leading them." His welcome everywhere left no doubts as to his popularity and his position as representative. The General had scored a capital point.

He now had to capitalise on it on the ground. Behind him, he left a team led by François Coulet, who had been promoted to Commissioner of the Republic in the liberated territories.

The next day, Coulet had a notice posted announcing his seizure of power in the name of the provisional government, and pronounced a first series of decrees. Over the following days, he relieved the Vichy government's *sous-préfet* and replaced him with Raymond Triboulet, a local landowner, a member of the Resistance and the Clandestine Liberation Committee. He also opened the way for the first newspaper in liberated France, *"La Renaissance du Bessin"*, whose first edition was dated 23rd June. A month later, in July, Roosevelt, drawing conclusions from the Bayeux visit, recognised de Gaulle's *de facto* authority over the liberated regions. That particular battle had been won.

De Gaulle addressing the inhabitants of Grandcamp, standing on a cart.

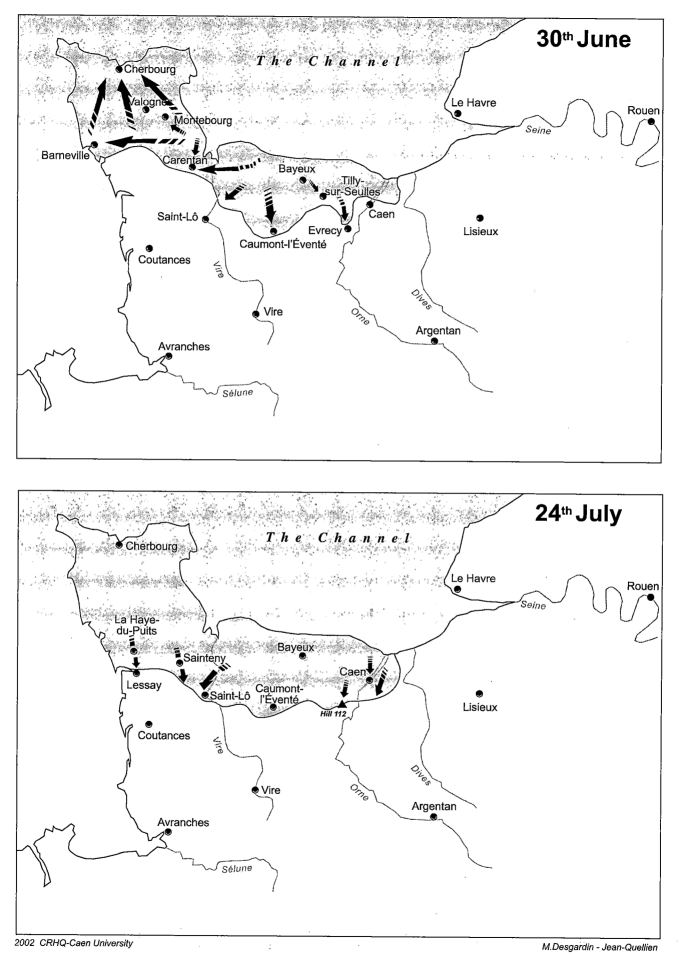

30th June

The Channel

Cherbourg
Valognes
Montebourg
Barneville
Carentan
Bayeux
Tilly-sur-Seulles
Caen
Saint-Lô
Evrecy
Lisieux
Caumont-l'Éventé
Coutances
Vire
Vire
Avranches
Argentan
Sélune
Le Havre
Rouen
Seine
Dives
Orne

24th July

The Channel

Cherbourg
La Haye-du-Puits
Bayeux
Lessay
Sainteny
Caen
Saint-Lô
Caumont-l'Éventé
Hill 112
Lisieux
Coutances
Vire
Vire
Avranches
Argentan
Sélune
Le Havre
Rouen
Seine
Dives
Orne

2002 CRHQ-Caen University

M.Desgardin - Jean-Quellien

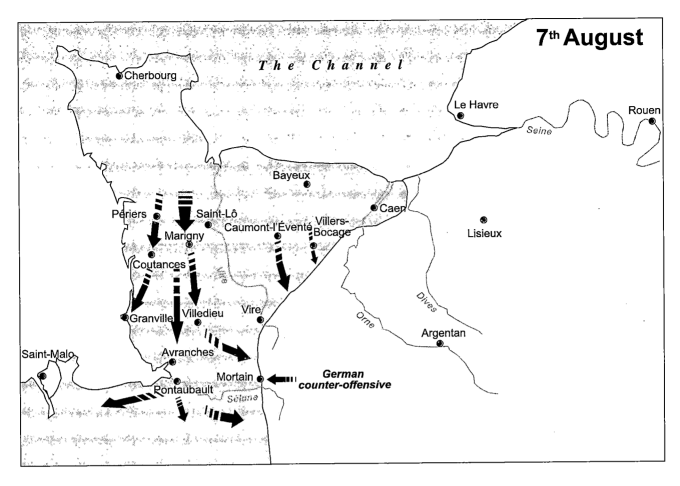

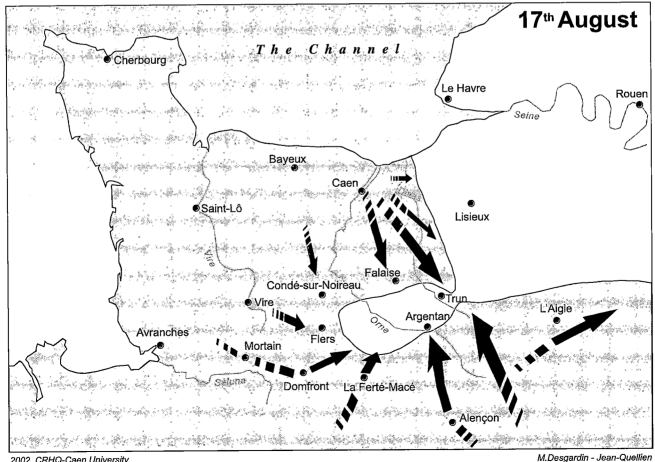

2002 CRHQ-Caen University

M.Desgardin - Jean-Quellien

Normandy 44 | **167**

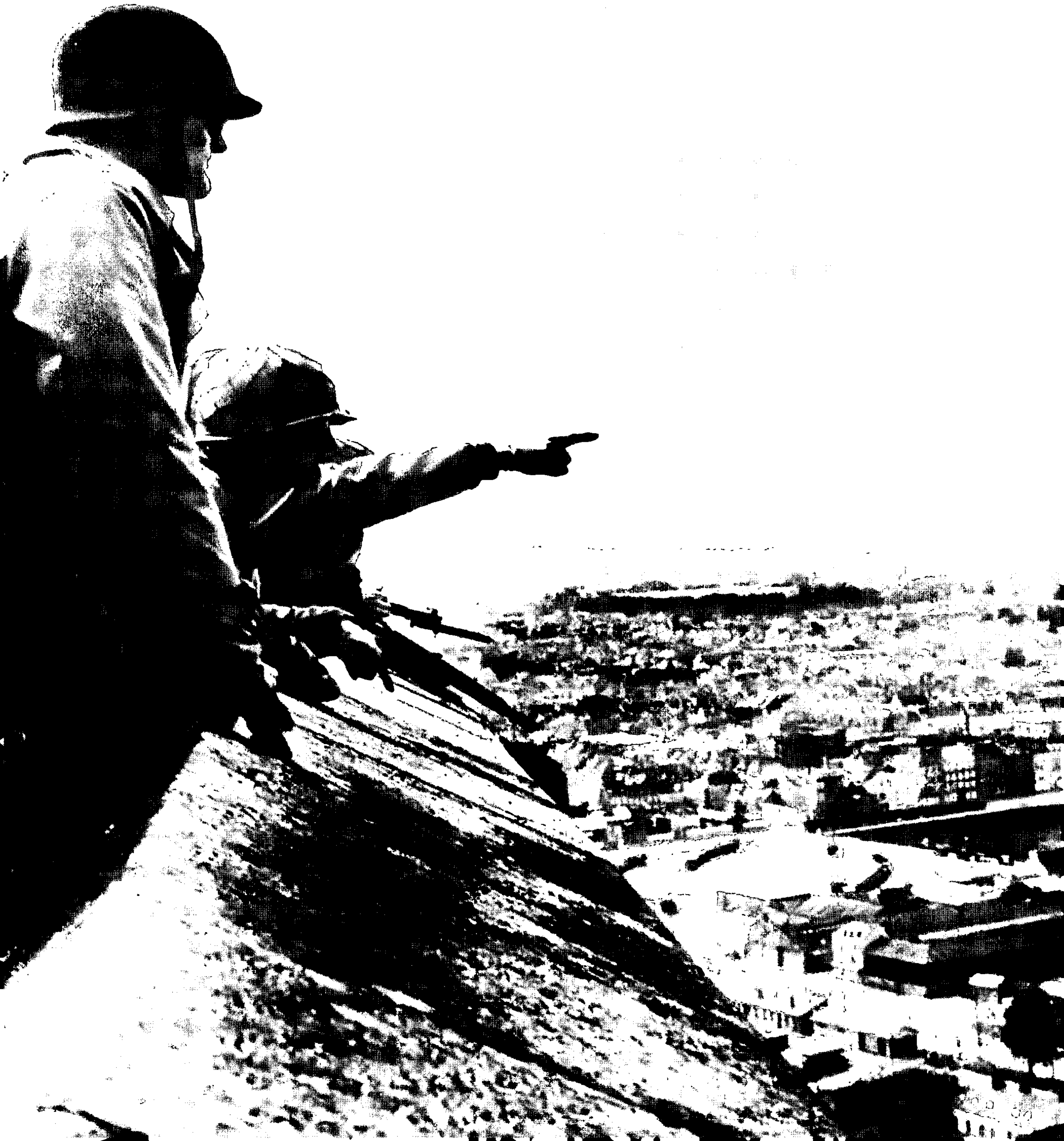

DESTINATION: CHERBOURG!

For Bradley, the Commander-in-Chief of the American troops, the time had come to launch the assault against Cherbourg, the strategic objective essential to Overlord's success.

Its port was to be used by ships coming directly from the United States, laden with the men and equipment necessary for the re-conquering of Europe.

Hitler himself was under no illusions and he ordered the town to be defended "*to the last man*".

The first assault, along the most direct route, the RN 13, was thwarted by determined German resistance in Montebourg, the siege of which was to last a fortnight, obliging part of the local population to stay hidden in their cellars or in the abbey. For the time being, another attack was launched where the enemy did not expect one, towards the western coast of the Cotentin.

American officers surveying the town from the Fort du Roule.

Near Montebourg, an abandoned 88-mm gun destroyed
by the German troops during their retreat towards Cherbourg.

Farmers in the Cotentin spontaneously helped the American troops by volunteering information.

Spearheaded by the 82nd Airborne, the Americans captured Saint-Sauveur-le-Vicomte on 16th June and reached the sea two days later, at Barneville. The peninsula was quickly and efficiently cut off. Forty thousand Germans were trapped. Their days of freedom were numbered. The ebullient General "Lightning Joe" Collins turned his 7th Army Corps northwards and set off apace. He advanced fast with three front-line divisions, liberated Briquebec then Valognes, or at least what was left of it, as *"Normandy's miniature Versailles"*, which had been bombarded several times since 6th June, had been transformed into nothing more than a desolate and mournful desert of rubble. During their advance, the Americans discovered a very large number of V1 launch pads, and even some V2s (in Brix), more or less badly damaged by the massive bombardments undertaken by the Allied aviation in the months leading up to the landings. By dint of its proximity to England, the Cotentin had been chosen as one of the sites where these rockets stuffed with explosives were to be based. Not one was to have been fired from here. The first V1 launched against London, during the night of 12th June 1944, was fired from the Nord Pas-

de-Calais coast. Thousands more were to follow. Roads and paths were jammed with long lines of lorries, jeeps, tanks, guns, under the gaze of country folk dumbfounded by such a display of military might. For the honest folk of the Cotentin, still snug in their old ways, this discovery of the sons of the world's largest industrial power was a shock. Everything about them was astonishing : from their ultra-modern equipment to their strange soluble coffee, their carefully packaged rations, their chewing gum and funny-smelling cigarettes.

Montebourg

Valognes.

VALOGNES CAPTURED BY TWO YANKEES

WILLIAM SPRINGER, WAR CORRESPONDENT FOR REUTERS

A JEEP DRIVER AND A LIEUTENANT WITH A ROSE BETWEEN HIS LIPS CALMLY CAPTURED THE TOWN OF VALOGNES, THE LARGEST YET TO HAVE FALLEN INTO ALLIED HANDS IN FRANCE, WITHOUT EVEN HAVING TO FIRE THEIR WEAPONS.

NO SHOTS WERE FIRED AND THERE WAS NO SIGN OF LIFE, OTHER THAN TWO OLD LADIES, A CAT AND AN EMPTY CANARY CAGE, WHEN, VALOGNES FELL AND SURRENDERED TO A PATROL OF TWO AMERICANS, LIEUTENANT DAVID L. ROOKS, FROM ZION (ILLINOIS) AND HIS DRIVER FROM AKRON (OHIO) PRIVATE JOHN P. SZWEJK.

THE GENERAL ATMOSPHERE OF THE PLACE WAS AS EERIE AS A TOMB WHEN I ENTERED VALOGNES, A FEW HUNDRED YARDS BEHIND THE VICTORIOUS PATROL. ROOKS AND SZWEJK DIDN'T LET OFF A SINGLE SHOT. BUT THEY DID CAPTURE FORTY OR SO GERMAN WORKERS WHO HAD BEEN SENT TO GIVE THEMSELVES UP BY A FRENCH FARMER. SZWEJK IMMEDIATELY SET THEM TO WORK ON A BRIDGE WHERE ONE OF THE ARCHES HAD BEEN BLOWN UP, IN ORDER TO GET TRAFFIC MOVING AGAIN. ROOKS ENTERED THE TOWN AT 10 O'CLOCK IN THE MORNING, CHEWING ON THE STEM OF A ROSE A FARMER'S WIFE HAD GIVEN HIM NEAR VALOGNES. THE TWO MEN REACHED THE TOWN CENTRE WITHOUT SEEING A SOUL AND ROOKS SUDDENLY STOPPED AND SHOUTED AS LOUDLY AS HE COULD. AN ECHO WAS THE ONLY REPLY HE GOT.

THE TOWN IS A SEA OF DESTRUCTION, UNDOUBTEDLY THE MOST DEVASTATED PLACE THAT THE AMERICANS HAVE SO FAR CAPTURED IN FRANCE. EVEN WORSE THAN MONTEBOURG, SAINT-SAUVEUR-LE-VICOMTE OR TRÉVIÈRES. NOT A SINGLE BUILDING HAS BEEN LEFT STANDING AND MOST ARE NO MORE THAN GAPING HOLES WHERE AMERICAN SHELLS HAVE LANDED.

MUCH OF RUE CARNOT, ONE OF THE TOWN'S MAIN STREETS, HAS COMPLETELY DISAPPEARED. ALL THAT REMAINS IS A SERIES OF HUGE CRATERS, SOME THIRTY FEET WIDE AND FIFTEEN FEET DEEP.

AS WE WALKED ALONG THE STREETS, WE HEARD NOTHING, EXCEPT FOR THE HEAVY THUD OF OUR BOOTS AND THE EERIE BANGING OF A SHUTTER BLOWING FROM TIME TO TIME IN THE WIND. THE ONLY SIGNS OF LIFE I SAW WERE A CAT ON A TABLE LAID FOR DINNER IN A HOUSE TOTTERING ON ITS FOUNDATIONS AND TWO ELDERLY WOMEN WITH TEARS IN THEIR EYES, WHO SHOUTED AFTER ME, "MERCI, MONSIEUR, MERCI" AS I LEFT TOWN.

One of Cherbourg's external defence bunkers exploding.

GIs just after the capture of the Fort du Roule.

Surrender of General von Schlieben, the commanding officer in Cherbourg.

The sea port, showing the effects of German sabotage.

On 21st June, the Americans clashed with the first lines of defence surrounding Cherbourg. They ordered the local commander, General von Schlieben, to surrender, but he refused, and gave orders for the total destruction of the port facilities. The first line of defence was pierced on 23rd June. Two days later, General Collins' men penetrated the town as battleships and cruisers began a duel of titans with the heavy German batteries. On the 26th, the Fort du Roule fell; General von Schlieben and Admiral Hennecke, the naval commander, left their underground bunker and surrendered. The remaining Germans defending the Arsenal held out a few hours more, before being sent to join their thousands of comrades who were already prisoners. Cherbourg was in American hands! The news made Hitler furious. The fortress should have held out for months! True, it had covered the sea and the sky with a formidable defensive array, but the same could not have

been said of the defences on land, whence no offensive was expected. Von Rundstedt paid the price of that day's crushing blow. He was replaced as Commander-in-Chief of the Western front by Marshal von Kluge, a veteran of the Eastern front, at the beginning of July. In Cherbourg itself, the bells were pealing with joy for the first time in four years. The mocking population watched the endless lines of beaten soldiers. The jubilant town welcomed its liberators with enthusiasm heightened by the fact that the town had not suffered greatly from the fighting. Up until then, the GIs had only come through ruins of towns, for the most part deserted. The atmosphere here was very different and the spirit of brotherhood swept through the town, helped along by some worthy bottles. On 27th June, thousands of Cherbourg's inhabitants cheered the victorious Generals, standing on the town hall steps. The Americans wished to lend the event a particular impact. Bradley was triumphant: *"It's a pleasure*

By the end of July, the port of Cherbourg was back in business.

to be able to say to the French: Here is your first major town back." That same day, from the heights above the town, the first programmes of Radio Cherbourg took to the airwaves, from the first station to broadcast in liberated France. There was one sore point: the port was in a lamentable state. The harbour was full of mines and the wrecks of ships sunk with dynamite, rails had been torn-up, cranes over-turned; there were traps all over the quays and the swing bridge had been sabotaged. But the specialist teams got down to work straight away, and strove without let-up to make it operational once again. They had been training for this task for many months. The Engineers toiled day and night without respite. Even if it was several months before Cherbourg had a fully operational port again, the first Liberty Ships from the United States began docking at the end of July. A few days later, PLUTO was in place. Thanks to this underwater pipe line leading from the Isle of Wight, the petro-leum terminal in Querqueville began to be supplied with fuel.

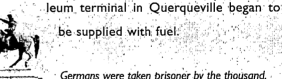

Germans were taken prisoner by the thousand.

In a liberated Cherbourg

CAEN, THE LINCHPIN OF THE BATTLE

The Germans had erected a barrier of fire and steel around Caen, which had stopped the Allies in their tracks and foiled hopes for a rapid deliverance. The 21st *Panzerdivision's* tanks, with reinforcements in the form of the tanks of the 12th *SS Panzerdivision Hitlerjugend*, resisted the British and Canadian offensives and kept them pinned down in the cornfields covering the plain. Caen had become the linchpin of the Battle of Normandy. Both camps knew that the town could open, or close, the road to the Seine and Paris. Caen had developed major strategic importance ... to the dismay of its inhabitants. A large proportion of its inhabitants had fled in haste right after the first aerial bombardment, taking blankets and a few precious souvenirs with them. Whole families joined the massive exodus to the south. Many others chose to take shelter in the quarries in Fleury-sur-Orne, Carpiquet and Mondeville. They were to live there like troglodytes for over a month.

The British and the Canadians fought hard for a whole month before capturing Caen.

The Germans surrounded Caen with a veritable barrage of fire and steel, with
their formidable armoured divisions. In the photograph, the Panzer Lehr.

In the majority of the areas of the centre of Caen, all life had come to a standstill. The only ones still there were the hundreds of dead, buried under the rubble that had once been their homes. The frightful stench of death hung over the city. Day and night, bombs and shells continued to fall, re-igniting huge fires that firemen and volunteers did their best to extinguish with their scanty equipment. The civil defence and the young people in the emergency teams worked non-stop to help the victims, whose number rose steadily. Thousands of Caen's inhabitants took refuge in the western part of the town, in the venerable Abbaye aux Hommes, invading the premises of the Lycee Malherbe and the Bon Sauveur hospital, too, where wounded victims of the conflagration arrived in their hundreds. On the ground, a red cross was hastily laid out using blood-soaked sheets; more were soon to be painted on the roofs. The British, warned of this last haven of life in the city centre by some brave envoy, did their utmost to avoid bombarding it.

But the *Caennais'* martyrdom was not yet near its end, because the British and the Canadians were meeting with ever stronger resistance. The German commander had brought his best divisions into action, notably the main body of his armoured divisions. Montgomery temporarily postponed the idea of a head-on confrontation, which he was afraid would be extremely costly in terms of both civilian and military human life, and set about launching a series of offensives to get round the city on the western side and attempt taking it from behind.

The first major failure was the blocking of General Graham's 50th Division by Bayerlein's *Panzer Lehr* at Tilly-sur-Seulles on 9th June. Well camouflaged and using the hedgerows to full effect, the German armour, accompanied by small infantry detachments, manoeuvred unceasingly and so established a defensive system that it was extremely difficult to break through. A lethal game of hide-and-seek raged for weeks in the countryside around Lingèvres, La Belle Epine, La Senaudière...

The village of Tilly-sur-Seulles,
captured and recaptured twenty times between 8th and 19th June.

An exploding munitions lorry near Fontenay-le-Pesnel, after a direct hit by a shell.

Tilly was captured by one side, then the other, changing hands twenty times in the space of ten days. In a manner of speaking, this was no longer Tilly-sur-Seulles, but Verdun-sur-Seulles. Many soldiers were lost to both camps, and 80 of the 750 villagers fell victim to the battle.

Montgomery then launched the 7th Armoured Division further to the right, in what seemed to be a sort of blind spot in the front. The famous Desert Rats, still aglow with their victories in Libya, advanced boldly at first and were on the point of taking the small town of Villers-

Bocage on 13th June, when they brutally made the acquaintance of the terrible Tiger tanks, steel behemoths weighing 55 tonnes and whose armour could withstand the impact of most types of shell, even when fired at short range. Suddenly appearing out of a neighbouring wood, a small group of these terrifying machines, rapidly joined by a few Panzer IVs, were enough to wipe out the British brigade spearheading the movement, and kick it unceremoniously out of Villers, constraining it to retreat over six miles.

The shadow of trench warfare loomed menacingly over the Normandy front.

25th June, beginning of operation Epsom. The Seaforth Highlanders (Scottish 15th Division) launched an offensive in the direction of the Odon.

At the end of June, Montgomery launched an large-scale offensive between Tilly-sur-Seulles and Caen, in the direction of the Odon. This was operation Epsom, involving 90,000 men. They reached and crossed the river on 27th June, but, shortly afterwards, the arrival of two German SS armoured divisions halted the British advance dead in its tracks at Hill 112, a hillock near Esquay-Notre-Dame, where fierce fighting, which was both indecisive and responsible for heavy casualties on both sides, was to last nearly a month. The battle was really getting bogged down. The fighting was being transformed into a war of position. Each day, the same names figured in the communiqués: Carpiquet, Hottot, Saint-Contest... On both sides, the soldiers were dug into deep trenches. Attacks followed counter attacks without any tangible result. The phantom shadow of the Great War hung over Normandy. The Anglo-Saxon press became impatient and began criticising General Montgomery bluntly, as did some Allied military chiefs, albeit less openly. Under pressure to act, Montgomery decided to revert to the principle of a frontal attack on Caen. It began on the evening of 7th July with a terrible Allied bombardment of the north of the city: 2,500 tonnes of bombs devastated a narrow zone between the Vaugeux district and the Place Saint-Sauveur, reducing the hitherto unscathed university to ashes and killing another 300 civilians. On the 8th, the Canadians ousted the SS from Buron and Authie, whereas the British beat down the last resistance around Lebisey.

By the evening, the Germans had begun to take flight. On 9th July in the morning, the Canadians captured Carpiquet, Saint-Germain-la-Blanche-Herbe, Venoix, La Maladrerie and penetrated Caen at last. The first soldiers reached the Place des Tribunaux towards midday, and were welcomed by the refugees who flocked out of the Abbaye-aux-Hommes and the Lycée Malherbe with sentiments we can imagine. Further east, the British were advancing slowly through streets made unrecognisable by the ruins characterising the city since 6th June. Here at last was the hour of liberation come to put an end to a month of suffering. There were, however, no cries of joy, nor delirious scenes - there was already too much mourning - but an intense emotion and a frank and heartfelt gratitude toward the Allies.

The Nebelwerfers launched salvoes of rockets with devastating effects.

rnfields around Caen.

Caen, 9th July: a Canadian patrol in the Rue Saint-Pierre.

Towards the end of the afternoon a brief patriotic ceremony was improvised in the little square in front of the school, where a tricolour flew from a lamp-post. The crowd, in which were visible the white helmets of the FFI of the Compagnie Scaramoni, sang a poignant Marseillaise.

But the Germans were still dug into the right bank, and reminded everyone of their presence by raining down shells from the Fleury-sur-Orne heights. They were to hold out there for ten days, until a renewed offensive finally dislodged them. On 19th July the Canadians, led by the FFI, took over the Vaucelles area of town. This time, Caen was completely liberated, but the enemy was still at its gates. Indeed, the massive offensive Goodwood, launched the previous day east of the city to free up the entrance to the plain, had been abortive. In spite of massive bombardments and the considerable means employed (three armoured divisions, comprising 900 tanks), the German defences, well and deeply spaced, held out. The British lost over 300 tanks in the operation, and only progressed a couple of miles. On the evening of 20th July they were anew at a halt, along a curving line running through Troarn, Frénouville, Bourgébus,

Old soldiers never die — they dig !

and Saint-André-sur-Orne. This failure rekindled the debate and Montgomery was once more the target of stinging criticism. There was certainly a great deal of unfairness in this, as the British Army had engaged the bulk and the finest of the enemy's forces, particularly and notably three-quarters of the armoured units active in Normandy. They thus made the Americans' task easier, at least in principal, as the latter, bogged down in the fighting in the hedgerows, did not seem capable of profiting from the situation.

Operation Goodwood, on 18th July, Cromwell tanks awaiting the signal to attack.

Refugees in
the Abbaye-aux-Hommes

"Hedgerow Hell"

Following the capture of Cherbourg and the Cotentin, Bradley brought his troops back down to the line running from Carentan to Portbail, in preparation for a new offensive towards the south. Somewhat drunk with their success in the northern Cotentin, the Americans had allowed themselves to become dangerously optimistic. They thought that the enemy would only offer purely formal resistance before retreating to Coutances. They were rapidly brought down to earth. The offensive, which was launched during the first days of July in driving rain, was making no headway. *"Maybe the Germans do not have much, but, boy! do they know how to use it!"* said one disenchanted observer. In fact, the Germans had received considerable reinforcements and had had the time to build very efficient defensive positions, defended by equally formidable troops, such as General Meindl's paratroops or the units from the *SS* Divisions *Das Reich* and *Götz von Berlichingen*.

Seven thousand GIs were killed or wounded in the capturing of the small town of Sainteny, between Carentan and Périers; ten thousand were put out of action before they took the Haye-du-Puits on 8th July, then Lessay, five miles away, ... a week later.

Every yard gained had cost one man!

The Americans entered Saint-Lô, the "capital of ruins", on 18ᵗʰ July.

Some companies had been reduced to a few dozen men. Their losses were to be even more fearful during the battle for Saint-Lô, stoutly defended by the storm-troopers dug into the hills north of the town. When he entered the "capital of ruins" with the 29ᵗʰ Division on 18ᵗʰ July, a war correspondent evoked the "valley of the shadow of death". He searched in vain for a house that was still intact and paused for a few moments in front of a cemetery that had been ploughed up by bombs and shells, where skeletons lay sprawled after having been ripped from their tombs. This war spared no-one, not even the departed.

The strategists in charge of Overlord had apparently anticipated everything, down to the smallest detail, with one glaring exception: the very specific configuration of the Normandy hedgerow country. The American war machine took its first steps into a maze of little fields surrounded by hedges and sunken lanes and its overwhelming material superiority became diluted in a landscape that was much more well suited to guerrilla action. Teams of gunners armed with *Panzerschreks* and *Panzerfausts*, hidden in the under-growth, destroyed tanks as if it were target practice.

The tanks exposed their un-armoured underbellies each time they rode over a hedge.

Support from the artillery and the tactical aviation, usually so decisive, was less useful here, given the impossibility of accurately identifying enemy positions. The Hedgerow warfare was first and foremost a batt-le of infantrymen, where the defender was in a posi-tion of force. Every embankment formed a natural fortification; every bush concealed a machine gun; every tree might contain a sniper. In this terrible man to man fight, the individual and tactical superiority of the German soldier was indisputable. "*We outclass them by ten to one in terms of infantry, fifty to one in terms of artillery, and in the air, our superiority is almost infinite... The Germans are resisting solely thanks to the sheer guts of their soldiers,*" said General Barton, com-mander of the 4ᵗʰ Division.

Plunged into this veritable hell, the GIs fell by the dozen, by the hundred, just to win a hedge that looked exactly like the one before, despairingly similar to those they had yet to conquer. Many became lost, or ran in panic, or deserted. Others mutilated or volun-tarily wounded themselves in order to escape a daily horror they could no longer cope with. Some succumbed to nervous depression or madness. The field hospitals were full and morale was sinking. *"We're progressing at a snail's pace,"* complained Bradley. *"The Germans are forcing us to pay an exorbitant price for every few miserable yards we win." "This bloody war could last ten years!"* added another American General.

This month of July 1944 was unquestionably the hardest and the darkest for the Allies. According to predictions, they should have liberated Brittany and reached the Loire by D-Day + 60, whereas they were still struggling on the line running from Saint-Lô to Caen. The front had only progressed a couple of miles and their losses had been frighteningly high. At this speed, it would have taken the Americans a month to reach Coutances.

Yet the fighting had not been easy on the Germans either. Fuel and ammunition was sent to them a little at a time. The tanks and men they received by way of reinforcement were ridiculous when compared to those profiting the Allies. By mid-July, they were fighting one to two, and were still lacking air support. Their forces began wearing down and out irreparably. Rommel did not attempt to hide the fact. In mid-July a few days before being seriously wounded by an

A Browning machine gun in position near Saint-Lô.

Allied fighter on a road in the Pays d'Auge, he had sent a prophetic report to his superiors: *"The situation is worsening steadily on the front in Normandy. Given the prevailing circumstances, we should expect that the adversary will soon succeed in breaching our defensive lines and penetrating deep into French territory. Our soldiers are fighting heroically everywhere, but this unequal struggle is nearing its end."*

The American 29th Division suffered very heavy losses in capturing Saint-Lô; some of the men taking time out from the memory....

German anti-tank guns covered the roads and pathways.

General Meindl's paratroops blended into the landscape in their camouflaged uniforms.

Near Lessay on 18th July.

The 2nd Armoured Division was the only American unit to supply its troops with camouflaged uniforms, sometimes a source of confusion with the Germans.

EVERY FIELD
IS A BATTLEGROUND

BILL DAVIDSON, YANK STAFF CORRESPONDENT

THIS IS A WAR OF HEDGEROWS, A STRANGELY LIMITED KIND OF WAR. HEDGEROWS ARE TALL, THICK BULWARKS LINING ALMOST EVERY ROAD AND EVERY FIELD. THEY ARE NOT NEW EMPLACEMENTS BUT ANCIENT DEMARCATION LINES, AND THEY HAVE BEEN PACKED DOWN INTO A CEMENT-LIKE HARDNESS BY THE PRESSURE OF CENTURIES. SOMETIMES, WHEN THE 88S AND THE 105S SCORE DIRECT HITS ON HEDGEROWS, THEY BLAST HOLES BARELY LARGE ENOUGH FOR TWO MEN TO SQUEEZE THROUGH.

FIGHTING IS FROM FIELD TO FIELD, AND FROM HEDGEROW TO HEDGEROW. YOU DON'T KNOW WHETHER THE FIELD NEXT TO YOU IS OCCUPIED BY FRIEND OR FOE. SOMETIMES YOU MAN THE FOUR HEDGEROWS BORDERING A FIELD AND HOLD IT AS YOU WOULD A TINY FORT SURROUNDED BY THE ENEMY. YOU RARELY SPEAK OF ADVANCING A MILE IN A SINGLE DAY; YOU SAY INSTEAD, "WE ADVANCED ELEVEN FIELDS". NORMALLY, NO-MAN'S-LAND IS THE WIDTH OF A SINGLE FIELD, BUT SOMETIMES ITS THE WIDTH OF A SINGLE HEDGEROW. THAT HAPPENS AFTER A LONG PERIOD OF FIRING, WHEN BOTH SIDES ARE TOO TIRED TO MOVE AND YOU CAN HEAR JERRIES TALKING A FEW FEET AWAY ON THE OTHER SIDE OF THE HEDGE. SOMETIMES YOU HOLD ONE END OF A FIELD AND THE ENEMY HOLDS THE OTHER AND YOU MANOEUVRE AROUND IN TWO- OR THREE-MAN PATROLS UNTIL EITHER YOU OR THE ENEMY IS THROWN OUT.

THIS KIND OF WAR IS PARADISE FOR THE SNIPER, THE AUTOMATIC WEA-PONS MAN, THE BAZOOKA MAN. CONVERSELY, IT'S DEATH ON TANKS AND ARMOURED CARS. THE MAN ON THE GROUND IS THE IMPORTANT JOE HERE, AND HE ISN'T FIGHTING BY THE BOOK.

THROUGHOUT THE FIGHTING, FRENCH FARMERS AND THEIR FAMILIES LIVE IN HOLES DUG INTO THEIR CELLARS WHILE THE FARMHOUSES ARE DES-TROYED OVER THEIR HEADS. WHEN THE FIGHTING PASSES OR A LULL BEGINS, THE CHILDREN COME OUT TO PLAY AND THEIR PARENTS BRING EGGS AND BUTTER TO THE GIS.

THESE LULLS ARE NECESSARY IN HEDGEROW WARFARE. AFTER HOURS SPENT ADVANCING THROUGH FIELDS, BOTH SIDES ARE SO WORN OUT THAT THEY MUST STOP TO REST, REGROUP AND GATHER UP THE DEAD AND WOUNDED. LULL, OF COURSE, IS A MISNOMER. SNIPERS KEEP WORKING, MORTAR AND ARTILLERY SHELLS PLOP DOWN AND PATROLS GO OUT AT NIGHT. BUT IT'S LIKE SUNDAY IN THE PARK BACK HOME COMPARED WITH WHAT WENT ON BEFORE.

THE TRAGEDY OF THE CIVILIANS ENSNARED IN THE BATTLE

The number of civilian victims of the Battle of Normandy, which was unknown or the subject of conjecture for a long time, has now been determined with precision. Not far from 20,000 men, women and children died during the fighting in the summer of 1944. It should be remembered that the soldiers of both camps fought in Normandy, not in a desert, as was the case in Libya, nor on a desert island, as they did in the Pacific, but in a region with a high density in terms of human population. Moreover, the duration of the battle (three months instead of the anticipated three weeks) only added to the death toll. At the peak of the intensity of the fighting, there were two million men engaged in battle, that is to say twice as many as the number of inhabitants in the departments of the Calvados and the Manche in which the fighting took place. This may give a clearer understanding of the ravages wreaked in a population brutally plunged into the heart of the war.

The refugees in the quarries in Fleury-sur-Orne, near Caen, welcoming their liberation after over forty days of living underground.

The rescue teams strove without cease to rescue the wounded and retrieve bodies from the ruins.

The Anglo-American armies advanced like a giant steam-roller, smashing and crushing everything in their way. With the intention of avoiding heavy losses in their ranks, the Allies' attacks were systematically preceded by terrible artillery barrages or air strikes. The shelling and bombing hit the German lines, of course, but did not spare the unfortunate civilians who did not always have the time or the opportunity to take effective cover. In the farms, villages and small towns, many built make-shift shelters, in anticipation of "really hard knocks". In many families, the father or the grandfather, a veteran of the Great War, had taken the initiative of digging trenches in the garden or the orchard, and of covering them with planks or bundles of wood. How many spent interminable hours inside them, huddled together in cramped misery, while the battle raged around them? These precautions were often pitifully inadequate in the face of the intensity of the cannonade and the bombardments.

A Douglas A-20 of the 9ᵗʰ US Air Force on a bombing mission over the Norman countryside.

The continuing air strikes

It is a fact that the most devastating air strikes against the Norman towns took place during the evening and the night of 6th June, but over the following days the Allied aircraft continued to wreak havoc and sow the seeds of death. The Allied high command was still obsessed with the necessity of hampering the movement of German troops to the front line. On 7ᵗʰ June in the afternoon, the flying fortresses dropped hundreds of bombs on Flers, Condé-sur-Noireau, Lisieux, Argentan, which had all been attacked the previous day, but also on Falaise, Avranches, L'Aigle and Valognes (bombed again on the 8ᵗʰ) adding hundreds to the list of civilian victims. Then the line of bombardment moved further inland, this time striking Alençon, Mayenne, Fougères, Rennes...

However, the ordeal of the Norman towns was still not over. As the battle progressed, several large towns experienced their share of destruction, such as Vimoutiers, Domfront, Périers, Saint-Hilaire-du-Harcouët, Thury-

Harcourt... In mid-June, Aunay-sur-Odon was crushed under bombs. Montgomery's staff had discovered a concentration of German armour in the sector and intended to block their advance. Nothing was left of this peaceful country town, except a tottering belfry rising out of a desert of ruins littered with the bodies of 150 inhabitants. During the night of 15ᵗʰ June, for identical reasons, Bomber Command pulverised the village of Evrecy, west of Caen, where 130 people out of a total population of 400 died in their sleep.

Immediately after the first Allied bombardments of the towns, tens of thousands of citizens fled to take refuge in the outlying farms, where they sheltered by the dozen, living and sleeping on the straw in the haylofts. The underground quarries, the caves and iron mine tunnels, which were numerous to the south of Caen, were also filled with their share of refugees. Many others chose the exodus.

Refugees near Saint-Lô. The bundles of wood were designed to catch shrapnel from shelling.

The Exodus

Whereas history has preserved the memory of the massive exodus of May and June 1940 which hit the north of France, it has given little attention to that of the summer of 1944 in Normandy. And yet it saw tens of thousands of men, women and children, old folks, babies and the sick take to the road: miserable cohorts heading into the unknown, on foot, by bicycle, in horse-drawn carriages, pushing shabby wheelbarrows or over-loaded prams, sometimes even with cows in tow. Their departure was the result of either spontaneous decisions taken by panicking populations fleeing the deluge of bombs and shells or, more frequently, evacuation orders given by the German army as it retreated. In July, whole villages were evacuated as the front rolled back towards them, only swelling the flood of refugees already on the roads.

Some fled without knowing where, tossed around by the fighting; others, more numerous, followed the itineraries established by the Vichy administration. For the inhabitants of the centre of the Manche, these led to the Mayenne, with a major staging point at Mortain. In the Calvados, the main route, leading from Caen and its surroundings, led to Trun in the Orne. We know that 45,000 people passed, midway, through the little village of Saint-Sylvain, where the Red Cross had set up a relay post. Some families undertook much longer journeys, finishing their frightful journey in the Vendée or in the Limousin.

This exodus was fraught with danger, as the Allied aviation, which filled the sky over Normandy, systematically machine-gunned and bombed the roads without always taking account of the difference between German mili-

The old folks from the hospice in Caen were carried to the quarries in Fleury-sur-Orne.

tary convoys and the unfortunate civilians. Many trage- dies resulted. The worst and most fatal happened not far from Vire. On 8th July, long lines of refugees from the area around Caumont-l'Éventé, riding on carts that were covered with white sheets, were stretched out along the road from Bény-Bocage to Vassy. In Saint-Charles-de- Percy, they had the misfortune to meet a German unit heading for the front. A squadron of P-47 Thunderbolts, fighter-bombers from the base in Cardonville, flew over unexpectedly and strafed the road and launched explo- sives. The toll was terrible: 27 dead, and many wounded, traumatised for life. The collaborationist press, which was more aggressive than ever, didn't miss the chance of exploiting the misery of the Normans by multiplying reports in an attempt to turn French public opinion against the Allies.

Aunay-sur-Odon, symbolic of the ordeal of the Normandy villages.

On the roads: the Exodus

THE BREAKOUT

Operation Cobra, launched by the Americans at the end of July, was to finally create the decisive breach in the German lines. Bradley had carefully elaborated his plan. A saturation bombing campaign over a restricted area was to be used to temporarily annihilate all existing defences and open the breach through which the Allied units would drive. For this operation, he chose the zone between the Chapelle-Enjuger and Hébécrevon, a few miles north of the main road linking Saint-Lô and Coutances.

"Cobra": the Americans strike!

A first attempt, on the 24th, turned into a disaster, when the bombers dropped their loads too far north, partly on the American front lines, killing or wounding 150 men. The operation was, however, renewed the following day. For three hours, 1,500 B-17 and B-24s churned up the target area, with support from medium bombers and fighter bombers using napalm. Once more, the GIs were put to the test, with over 100 killed and 500 wounded, so much so that Eisenhower forbade any subsequent use of heavy bombers as ground support.

30th July: American tanks reached Avranches, achieving a breakthrough of some 40 miles in one week.

The start of the breakout on 27ᵗʰ July in Marigny.

But this time, the Germans were not spared. On the contrary, the *Panzer Lehr*, which had just arrived in the sector, was literally pulverised. Panzer tanks weighing 45 tonnes were thrown into the air by the force of the explosions, flipped over and broken into pieces like so many children's toys. Infantrymen were buried alive in the trenches or in their shelters. The rare survivors, stunned, gave up without a fight or ran away. General Bayerlein, who escaped miraculously, admitted that it had been the *"worst experience of my existence"*. In answer to his superiors, who urged him to hold on at any price, he replied: *"You can be sure that my men will not retreat a single inch, for they are all dead!"*

For all that, the American infantry's task was not a piece of cake. All through the day on the 25ᵗʰ, it had to fight hard to open the passage for the armour, while the engineers' bulldozers prepared the terrain for tanks, filling in craters. On 26ᵗʰ July, General Collins'

7ᵗʰ Corps, with support on its right flank from Middleton's 8ᵗʰ Corps and on the left from Corlett's 19ᵗʰ Corps, progressed six miles capturing Saint-Gilles then Canisy after having crossed the Coutances-Saint-Lô road. Fissures began to appear right across the German front, which was now no more than a simple crust without any depth. It fell apart the next day. The American armoured divisions rolled unstoppably westwards and southwards. Marigny, Lessay and Périers were captured during the day. Coutances was liberated on the 28ᵗʰ by General "Tiger Jack" Wood's 4ᵗʰ Armoured Division, spearheading the cavalcade.

The Germans attempted to stem the flood by setting up strong-points at crossroads, but the American tanks were now crossing fields, busting through hedges with easy nonchalance. Bradley had kept Sergeant Curtis Cullins' ingenious invention secret: it was a jaw of steel teeth cut from the obstacles salvaged on the beaches and mounted on the front of the tanks. At 15 or 20 mph, the Sherman tanks went through the hedgerows like hack-saws through gristle. Whole German units were surrounded, as was the case in the Roncey pocket, and were not always able to escape. Nearly 5,000 men were killed or captured there, and a mass of equipment was abandoned. Others ran away. The weight of two long months of fierce and relentless fighting fell brutally on these shaken and demoralised soldiers. Russians and their comrades from Alsace, who had been conscripted by force into the Wehrmacht, lost no time in deserting; they hastily swapped their "field-grey" uniforms for civilian clothing with the villagers, who were only too delighted to see the distress and confusion of the routed Occupier. Thousands of men were captured, disarmed and left where they were found because there was no time to take them to a camp. Von Choltitz, commander of the 84th Corps, vainly tried to reconstitute new lines of defence, which became obsolete before they had been completed. All his operational bases were neutralised or overrun in rapid

The body of a German soldier, brutal symbol of a routed army.

succession. He suffered from a cruel lack of infantry. Here and there administrative staff, orderlies, cooks and even nurses were requisitioned and ordered to take up arms, but there was no stopping the Americans now. They were caught up in the momentum of a veritable cavalry charge, like something out of the pages of an earlier history.

Destroyed and abandoned German equipment in the Roncey pocket.

Coutances, liberated on 28th July.

Stops were very frequent for the liberators.

On 30th July, Gerow's 6th Armoured Division crossed Bréhal and passed by Granville without stopping. That same evening, Wood, who was still spearheading the charge, captured Avranches, thus cutting off the enemy's retreat, and throwing it into confusion. On the following day, he succeeded in taking the bridge over the Sélune at Pontaubault intact, thus preserving the single most important strategic point on the road west to Brittany. In under a week, Bradley's troops had advanced nearly 40 miles and taken 18,000 prisoners. The battle had suddenly taken on a very different complexion. The breakout had been achieved. War of attrition could now give way to mobile warfare. Since the end of July, the general staff of the *Wehrmacht* had, with Hitler's approval, begun to deploy some of the divisions stationed in Picardy and the Pas-de-Calais in the direction of Normandy. This initiative was as tardy as it was by then pointless. They were torn to pieces en route by the Allied aviation and reached the front sorely depleted and incapable of reversing the course of events.

As they progressed, the American troops were ever more enthusiastically welcomed.

The battle in the hedged farmland of the "Bocage"

On 1st August, the Americans reorganised their operation before engaging the next phase of the battle. Patton's hour had come. As planned, he took command of the newly formed 3rd Army and launched resolutely into the fray without more ado. In less than three days seven divisions, that is to say about 100,000 men and 10,000 vehicles passed through the narrow breach south of Avranches, before fanning out. One of these army corps marched on Brittany, a second headed for the Loire, and the third set its sights on Le Mans. Bradley was promoted to the command of the 12th Army Group and his successor, Hodge, and his 1st Army were meanwhile making difficult progress towards the east, driving up the valleys of the See and the Sélune. The offensive was a combined operation with the British 30th Corps, which had launched an attack southwards from Caumont-l'Éventé within the framework of operation Bluecoat. The hilly Bocage landscape, its narrow and twisting roads and its dense vegetation hampered the Allies' progress. The battle became characterised by sporadic skirmishing involving small units. The Germans retreated slowly, fighting especially hard to keep control of the crossroads, the sunken lanes and the isolated farms, scattering mines and traps behind them as they went.

On 2nd August, the Americans entered Percy after five days of fighting, liberated Villedieu, Juvigny-le-Tertre and Saint-Hilaire-du-Harcouët, and entered Mortain on the following day. The British captured Villers-Bocage and what was left of Aunay-sur-Odon. After the difficult struggle involved in conquering Mont-Pinçon, they moved in the direction of Vire, by the east, but encountered fierce resistance from the 9th and 10th *Panzerdivisions SS* around Estry and Chênedollé.

The meeting of two worlds: an ultra-modern army and old country-women straight out of the 19th Century.

Mortain: the failure of the last German spurt of effort

Then came the thunderbolt. The Germans launched a substantial armoured counter-offensive on either side of Mortain on the morning of 7th August. Operation Lüttich's every detail had been planned in the Wehrmacht's central staff headquarters, in total disregard for the opinions of the military commanders on the ground. The objective, defined by Hitler in person, was clear. Smash through the American lines and drive to the Baie de Mont-Saint-Michel, 20 miles to the east, cutting off the Avranches bottle-neck at the same time. Patton's troops engaged in Brittany and in the Maine would be cut off from supply lines and isolated, and would fall like ripe fruit.

With this objective in mind, four Panzerdivisions with infantry support were very secretly deployed. Taking advantage of the element of surprise and the morning fog, the Panzers broke through and advanced five or six miles in certain sectors. Mortain, which had been heavily bombarded by the Lufwaffe during the night, was recaptured by the Germans. The 30th US Infantry, on guard in the town, took the brunt of the attack and had to pull out. Some of its units found themselves surrounded, such as the famous "lost battalion", isolated and besieged at the summit of Hill 314, a hill east of the town. It heroically resisted the SS's repeated attempts to dislodge it for six days and six nights. Nevertheless, the Americans were not long in recovering.

On 7th August at the beginning of the afternoon, the fog lifted at last and the battle took on a new complexion. The sky filled with a pack of fighter-bombers that fell on

Operation Bluecoat: columns of British armour launching the offensive in the Bocage.

A brief moment of respite for two gunners in an abandoned farm in the Bocage.

the armoured columns like ravening wolves on the fold, attacking with guns and their devastating salvoes of rockets. The waves of Typhoons followed each other in rapid succession. They only returned to base to fill up on fuel and ammunition before flying straight back to swoop down on their prey again. This infernal carousel lasted about eight hours; eight hours of nightmare for the German armoured divisions, nailed down, with 150 tanks already out of action. By the evening of the 7th, it was obvious they had failed. The Führer, however, remained obstinate for several days, railing against his Generals, whom he accused of ineptitude... or treason. Von Rundstedt's successor, von Kluge, was not to last long. He was dismissed shortly thereafter, replaced by Marshal Model, and chose to take his own life. Hitler had just played his last trump card in Mortain. He had lost it.

Soldiers of the British 43rd Infantry Division in difficult terrain.

The failure of the Mortain counter-offensive. The remains of a German column destroyed by the Allied fighter-bombers.

German prisoners near Avranches.

VICTORY

The risky counter-attack at Mortain was to precipitate the German collapse and the end of the Battle of Normandy. Bradley and Montgomery decided not to waste any time in exploiting the new situation. By means of a large circular movement, they could trap the enemy divisions that had been imprudently advanced westwards.

The last bloody act in the Falaise Pocket

Instructions were immediately given accordingly. Haislip's American 15th Corps, which had entered Le Mans on 9th August received orders to move northwards fast, spearheaded by the American 5th Armoured Division and recently landed General Leclerc's French 2nd Armoured Division. On the 12th, the latter took Alençon by surprise and drove through town in an atmosphere of riotous joy before moving rapidly on Écouché, which was captured the following day, then on to Argentan. Meanwhile, Montgomery had re-launched the offensive south of Caen. Overstretched by the departure of its armoured units that had been sent to Mortain, the German defence was broken, but not without some difficulty. The enemy although retreating, was still capable of inflicting severe damage on its adversaries, as was the case at Estrées-la-Campagne, where a regiment of Canadian armour was severely trounced. As they retreated, they threw the village populations out of their homes, forcing them to take to the road as evacuees.

The Polish 1st Armoured Division participated in the final phase of the Battle of Normandy.

General Leclerc and the French 2nd Armour in Fleuré, not far from Argentan.

There were scenes of joy in Alençon, liberated on 12th August by the Frenchmen of the 2nd Armoured Division.

With determined energy and by mounting attack on attack (operations Totalize I and II, Tractable), the Canadians and General Maczek's Polish I st Armoured Division, freshly engaged on the front, were approaching Falaise. The town, which was defended with savage and tenacious desperation by a handful of the fanatical *SS Hitlerjugend*, was finally tamed on 17th August. It only remained to link up with the Americans, who were now at the gates of Argentan.

The German 5th Armoured Army and 7th Army – or at least all that was left of them, about 150,000 men – were in the process of being surrounded. On 16th August, Hitler at last gave the order for a general withdrawal towards the Seine, a movement which had already begun. Since the 14th, indeed, units were retreating in droves everywhere and trying to find a way back east. The commanders tried above all to save what was left of their armoured divisions. The bulk of the infantry, dispersed in the Bocage and left to fend for itself, made an increasingly disorderly dash for the gap in Allied lines between Argentan and Falaise, that was growing narrower by the day.

Under combined pressure from the Americans in the south, the British in the west and the Canadians and Poles in the north, the vice slowly but inexorably tightened between Argentan and Trun, where the last act of the tragedy was to unfold. From all sides, the Allied artillery pounded away at the enemy, caught in a noose and thrown into confusion. The retreat gradually turned into a rout, a hopeless flight towards the "corridor of death", where packs of fighter-bombers wallowed in a pitiless carnage. Smoking carcasses clogged up the roads, maddened horses ran hither and thither and hundreds of bodies lined the lanes and fields, surrounded by the clutter of abandoned weapons and equipment. As the net was only closing slowly, because of a series of disagreements between the Allies, several tens of thousands of men managed to escape from the pocket; but on the morning of 21st August, it was definitively closed after a dramatic bout of fighting around the little villages of Chambois, Saint-Laurent, Trun and Tournai-sur-Dives, where the rearguard of the escapees from the infernal "cauldron" were to be confronted simultaneously by Americans, French, Canadians, British and Poles, symbolically gathered in this place where the German defeat in Normandy was finally confirmed.

In the corridor of death

After much fierce fighting, the Anglo-Americans mastered Argentan, bitterly defended by the 116th Panzer.

The battle in the "Falaise Pocket" was not really a "Stalingrad in Normandy", as has been said, considering that 100,000 Germans succeeded in escaping the Allies between 12th and 20th August. They did, however, have to abandon 400 tanks, 1,000 field guns, 2,000 motorised vehicles, 50,000 prisoners and 6,000 dead.

The rotting bodies of men and animals had been shoved into messy, stinking heaps along the narrow sunken lanes, in the midst of the debris of smashed or burnt-out vehicles. The vision was hallucinatory: teams of men equipped with gas masks ran through this scene, firing into the gas-bloated carcasses of cattle and horses. *"This is one of the greatest scenes of carnage of the war,"* said Eisenhower on visiting the battlefield. *"One could go literally hundreds of yards walking over nothing but dead and putrefying flesh, in a deathly silence, in the middle of luxuriant countryside where all life had brutally ceased, leaving only destruction and death."*

The Wehrmacht's retreat

The German troops that had escaped the disaster of the "Falaise Pocket" retreated towards the Seine, harassed on all sides now by detachments of the FFI. The Germans took cruel revenge on all those they captured, shooting them on the spot. Sometimes they even took it out on the population. In Tourouvre, the SS savagely murdered seventeen people guilty of having too noisily demonstrated their joy at the approach of their liberation. The British advanced fast across the Pays d'Auge and liberated Lisieux on 25th August. The town had been sorely tried by the bombardments, in which a thousand of its inhabitants had perished. The basilica, which was filled with refugees, gathered around the venerable Mother Agnès, a sister of Saint-Theresa's, had miraculously escaped harm. Further north, Colonel Piron's Belgian Brigade and the Dutch "Princess Irene" Brigade, in concert with the British 6th Airborne, drove along the coast, liberating Cabourg, Dives, Trouville-Deauville, and finally Honfleur. To the south, the Canadians were in Bernay, and the Americans in Evreux, Louviers, and Elbeuf.

Although they were trapped between the advancing Allies and the Seine, the bridges over which had been destroyed, the Germans were to manage to escape. The attempt to close them into a new pocket was launched without much conviction. They crossed the river however they could, on ferries, on rafts, in amphibious vehicles, in boats, and sometimes even by swimming. A bridge of boats was cobbled together at Poses, near Elbeuf, and in Rouen, the relatively undamaged railway bridge was hastily patched up.

In total, and according to an official British report, the Germans managed a veritable exploit: they succeeded in saving 240,000 men, 30,000 vehicles and nearly 150 tanks. Their material losses were limited to about 4,000 vehicles and fifty-odd tanks, destroyed by air strikes or simply lacking fuel. However, once they had reached the opposite bank, it was impossible for them to consider mounting any resistance worth speaking of, and those remnants of a drained army had no option other than to retreat rapidly in the direction of the Reich, without looking back.

The 11,000-strong garrison in Le Havre stayed put, not intending to give up without a fight. The Germans had transformed the town into a formidable entrenched camp, bristling with heavy artillery batteries and full of concrete bunkers and pillboxes.

A brief instant of relaxation in Falaise, which fell to the Canadians on 17th August.

EVERYTHING IS RIPPED UP AND SLASHED OPEN

ALAN MOOREHEAD, *DAILY EXPRESS*

THE FALAISE POCKET – OR SUCH OF IT AS REMAINS – WAS FINALLY SEALED OFF LATE YESTERDAY, WHEN THE CANADIAN AND AMERICAN ARMIES JOINED HANDS IN THE WOODS OF CHAMBOIS, NEAR ARGENTAN. ALL THROUGH TODAY THE LIFE WAS SLOWLY SQUEEZED OUT OF THAT TRAPPED REMNANT OF VON KLUGE'S SEVENTH ARMY. THE ALLIED ARMOUR AND INFANTRY WENT OVER IT AND ROUND IT, AND THEN, MEETING ON THE EASTWARD SIDE, PUSHED ON AGAIN. AS YET I HAVE BEEN ABLE TO SEE ONLY A TINY CORNER OF THIS IMMENSE BATTLEFIELD. BUT I FANCY THE VIEW FROM HERE IS FAIRLY TYPICAL OF WHAT THE ADVANCE LOOKS LIKE.

WE HAVE DRIVEN THROUGH FALAISE (STILL BURNING AND WALLS FALLING ACROSS THE ROADWAYS) IN THE FRESH MORNING, WITH ALL THE COUNTRYSIDE WASHED BY THE OVERNIGHT SHOWERS.

TWO LANES LEAD OFF EITHER SIDE OF THE MAIN ROAD. BOTH ARE JAMMED WITH SMASHED GERMAN VEHICLES AND DEAD HORSES.

I SUPPOSE THE WRECKAGE IS SO AWFUL BECAUSE IT IS CONFINED IN SUCH A NARROW SPACE BETWEEN THE HEDGES AND BECAUSE DEATH CAME SO QUICKLY TO THE GERMANS.

EVERYTHING IS RIPPED UP, AND RIPPED AND SLASHED OPEN, BITS OF MOTORCYCLES TUMBLED ONTO OVERTURNED LORRIES AND STAFF CARS AND WOODEN CARTS, GUNS WITH THEIR NOZZLES DUG INTO THE DIRT AND ALL THE GROUND AROUND MATTED WITH PAPERS AND CLOTHING AND SODDEN BITS OF TORN CANVAS AND WEBBING. THERE ARE TWO GERMANS LYING FACE DOWNWARD ON THE LEFT. AN IMMENSELY FAT GERMAN SERGEANT, WITH HIS YELLOW HANDS FOLDED OVER HIS STOMACH, IS UNDER THE HEDGE WHERE HE TRIED VAINLY TO CRAWL FOR SHELTER AND CONCEALMENT BEFORE HE DIED. ALL AROUND ARE HORSES AND CATTLE – MORE AND MORE CARCASSES IN THE ORCHARD, OVER BY THE HAYSTACK AND THROUGH THE WHEAT. ONE'S STOMACH TURNS AT THE STENCH. ONE COULD WRITE OF FIFTY INCIDENTS OF THIS DAY AND NOT EXHAUST THE STORY.

THE GERMANS CAUGHT IN THE GRASS FIRES BURNING UP TO THE EDGES OF THE RUINED VILLAGES. THE BATTERY OF GERMAN FIELD GUNS THAT SURRENDERED INTACT TO A HANDFUL OF BRITISH SIGNALLERS, WHO WERE LAYING DOWN A LINE FOR GENERAL DEMPSEY.

THE BEWILDERED GERMAN BAND THAT WAS CAUGHT WITH ITS CONCERTINAS AND TRUMPETS IN AN ORCHARD NEAR HERE. THE TOMMIES RIDING FORWARD BAREBACK ON CAPTURED HORSES. THE SOLITARY ARAB IN A RED FEZ CAUGHT SIGHT OF IN A PRISONER'S VAN. THE OFFICERS GETTING INTO ABANDONED GERMAN STAFF CARS AND PUSHING ON WITH THE PURSUIT.

EVERYTHING IS IN MOTION.

The Germans crossed the Seine however they could at the end of August.

The fortress was protected on three sides by the sea, the Seine and a flooded valley. The only access road, to the north, was protected by an impressive defensive system, well placed and deep, including a gigantic anti-tank trench and tens of thousands of mines.

The assault ran the risk of being fatal for General Crocker's British 1st Army Corps, so the RAF was called in to assist them. To avoid a carnage, the local German commander offered to allow the civilians to leave, but the British refused, thinking that they could in this way constrain the enemy to surrender. The outcome was not as they hoped. The sixty thousand inhabitants of Le Havre who were hostage to this dramatic game of poker were about to go through hell. On 5th and 6th September there was a massacre. The centre of the town was destroyed with explosive bombs and incendiary devices.

On the evening of the 10th, Crocker gave the go-ahead for the Astonia offensive. Two infantry divisions and three armoured brigades, preceded by special tanks, launched the offensive, under a thunderous artillery barrage. The assault has become the stuff of legend due to its precision and speed of execution. The "flail" tanks opened paths through the minefields while the terrifying flame-throwing "crocodiles" instilled dread in the hearts of the defenders. Le Havre was liberated on 12th September, but at what a price! Around 2,000 civilians had died in the ruins of the town, 85% of which had been flattened.

Meanwhile, no longer encountering any resistance ahead, Montgomery had reached the Belgian border and libera-

Le Havre, the last victim of the Battle of Normandy.

ted Brussels on 4th September. The Americans left a few divisions to clean up in Brittany, with support from the *"franc-tireurs"*, and fanned out between the Ardennes and the Loire. On 25th August, Gerow's 5th Army Corps, with Leclerc's 2nd Armoured Division at the head of the column; liberated Paris whose population had risen in insurrection several days previously. Six days later, Patton's troops were at Verdun. Finally, while the Falaise Gap was dwindling and the pocket closing, the Allies had struck another blow, this time in Provence. On 15th August, Franco-American forces landed between Cavaliare and Saint-Raphaël. General Sodenstern's army, which had been weakened by the departure for Normandy of a number of divisions, did not last long. Rapidly General de Lattre de Tassigny's French 1st Army and Patch's 7th Army swarmed up the Rhone and Durance valleys. Their progress was so swift that it began to resemble pursuit. Lyon was liberated on 3rd September. For its part, the German 1st Army evacuated the southwest, to avoid becoming surrounded, under constant harassment from the FFI.

Sallenelles on 16th August: Colonel Piron's Belgian 1st Brigade preparing to push towards Cabourg. It participated in the liberation of the "Côte Fleurie", as far as Trouville-Deauville.

The French Resistance, here in Écouché, worked with the Allies.

With the exception of a few pockets of resistance on the Atlantic seaboard and along the Channel coast, the enemy had been almost entirely chased out of France. Only the Vosges and Alsace were still in German hands. Leclerc's entry into Strasbourg on 23rd November, and de Lattre's capture of Colmar on 2nd February 1945 were only won after several months of determined fighting. Germany capitulated three months later, thus putting an end to the Third Reich.

Tens of thousands of German soldiers were captured in the Falaise Pocket.

Saint-Lô

THE MARTYRDOM OF NORMANDY, THE PRICE PAID FOR THE LIBERATION OF FRANCE

According to the plans of operation Overlord, the liberation of Normandy should have been achieved in three weeks. Four times as many were to have elapsed before that objective was attained. The Allies had struggled, and had lost over 200,000 men in the Battle, 37,000 of them dead. But the Germans had lost the bulk of their forces in the West in the confrontation: 400,000 were made prisoner, killed or wounded, along with a very substantial proportion of their equipment and their tanks. They had resisted for three months, right up to the extreme limit of their capacities, before collapsing totally. As a result, the liberation of France was as rapid and easy as that of Normandy had been long, difficult and costly.

Nearly 20,000 civilians had died. Caen, Lisieux, Coutances, Saint-Lô, Vire to name but a few were on the long list of towns that had been laid waste; peaceful villages had been blotted out. Economic activity had been very considerably disrupted. Artistic and cultural treasures were gone forever. Normandy was to carry the scars of war for many years.

Its ordeal was the ransom to pay for national liberation. It is fitting today that no-one forget that fact, as it is fitting that the sacrifice of a region and its inhabitants be forever linked in our memories to the sacrifice of those young men who came from over the Channel and over the Atlantic, and who now rest in peace forever in this land they came to liberate.

Jean Quellien

PHOTOGRAPHIC CREDITS

Departmental archives of the Calvados : pp. 15 (b), 29 (tr), 59, 87 (t), 145, 196, 204, 208 (m), 209 (m) ;

Departmental archives of the Calvados / J. Quellien collection : pp. 4, 37 (b) ;

Associated Press : p. 46 ;

Atypik : Cover (tl) ;

Bundesarchiv, Koblenz : pp. 6 (h), 28, 30-31, 32,34,35,36 (tl & b), 37 (t), 38-39, 40, 41 (b) 42, 43, 44, 48, 129 (tl), 144, 185, 186 (t), 239 (bl) ;

J. Benamou collection : pp. 95, 100 ;

Caen Memorial collection : pp. 9 (m & b), 49 (t & m), 125, 201 (ml), 207 (t) ;

Caen Memorial collection / R. Shall : p. 7 ;

Caen memorial collection / P & G Custom : p. 58 (t) ;

ONAC 14 collection / Hettier de Boislambert : p. 165 ;

B. Paich collection : pp. 36 (tr), 103 (b) ;

J. Quellien collection : pp. 9 (t), 27, 45, 49 (tr & b) ;

DITE : pp. 20, 23 (t), 50, 67 (bl), 73 (t), 79 (m), 81 (t), 142, 150 (t), 153 (bl), 201 (br & tl), 205, 212, 213 (b), 221 (h), 225, 226 (m), 234 (b) ;

DR : pp. 76, 94, 130-137, 157 (b), 177 (b), 179 (mr), 196-197 (background), 209 (tl), 216 (t), 233 (t) ;

ECPAd : pp. 6 (b), 24, 29 (tl), 41 (t), 138, 140-141, 146, 182, 186 (tr), 192, 232, 239 (br) ;

Imapress : pp. 84-85, 129 (tr) ;

Imperial War Museum London: pp. 2-3, 10, 12, 13, 14, 15 (t), 16, 51, 52 (tr), 53-57, 58 (b), 60-62, 65, 66 (t & b), 67(tl), 70, 89 (tl), 103 (t), 106, 116, 119-122, 147, 149 (b), 150 (bl), 151, 153 (tl & br), 156, 157 (hl), 158, 160, 162-164, 183, 184 (t & br), 186-187 (b), 189 (b), 190 (b), 191, 207 (b), 208 (b), 209 (tr), 219, 220, 226 (t & b), 227, 230, 234 (t), 239 (tl) ;

Imperial War Museum / J. P. Benamou collection : pp. 64, 73 (b), 104-105, 118, 128, 129 (b) ;

Memorial / CRHQ / M. Desgardins / J. Quellien : maps ;

Mémorial du Marechal Leclerc de Hautecloque et de la Libération de Paris and the J. Moulin museum / Ville de Paris : p. 224 ;

National Archives Canada : Cover (tr), pp. 52 (tl), 66 (m), 67 (r), 72, 74, 108, 110-114, 124, 126, 139, 153 (mr), 180, 184 (bl), 188, 189 (t), 190 (t), 191 (mr), 202, 222, 229, 233 (b) ;

National Archives USA : Cover (b), pp. 21 (t), 22, 23 (b), 26 (t), 29 (b), 68-69, 78 (background), 80 (b), 81 (b), 82, 86, 88, 89, 92, 96-99, 102, 148, 149 (t), 150 (br), 152, 153 (tr & ml), 154, 157 (tr), 159, 168, 170-176, 177 (t), 178-179, 194, 195, 197, 198, 200, 201 (bl & tr), 206, 208 (t), 209 (b), 210, 213 (t), 214-215, 216 (b), 218, 221 (b), 227 (bl), 228, 235-237, 239 (tr) ;

National Archives USA / J. P. Benamou collection : pp. 18, 21 (b), 80 (t), 87 (b), 90, 127, 217 ;

National Archives USA / Caen Memorial collection : Cover (bl), p. 1 ;

Olivier Houdart / Dollar : Cover (background) ;

French Ministry for ex-servicemen : pp. 8, 26 (b) ;

THE LONGEST NIGHT

TUESDAY 6ᵀʰ JUNE 1944 ENTERS HISTORY

THE FOUR-YEAR WAIT

THREE MONTHS OF FIGHTING IN NORMANDY

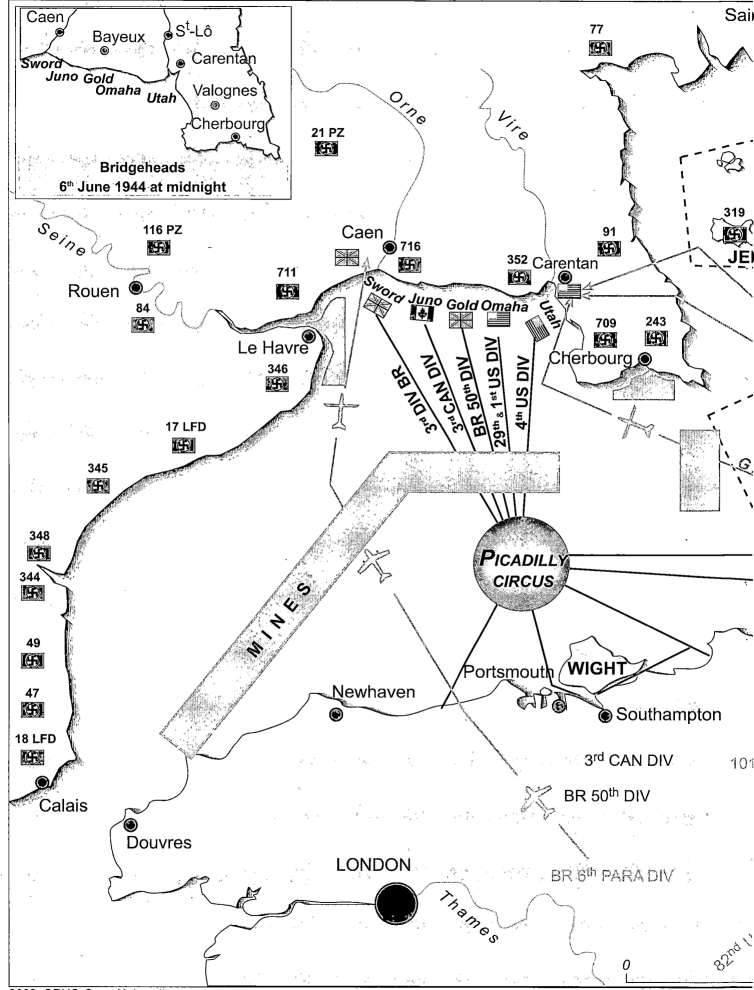

Caen
Bayeux
S^t-Lô
Carentan
Sword
Juno Gold
Omaha Utah
Valognes
Cherbourg

**Bridgeheads
6th June 1944 at midnight**

Orne
Vire
Seine

77
21 PZ
319
JE

116 PZ
Caen ● 716
91
352 Carentan

Rouen ●
711
709 243
Cherbourg ●

84
346

Le Havre

Sword Juno Gold Omaha Utah

17 LFD

3rd DIV BR
3rd CAN DIV
BR 50th DIV
29th & 1st US DIV
4th US DIV

345

348
344

**PICADILLY
CIRCUS**

M I N E S

49

Portsmouth **WIGHT**

47

Newhaven
● Southampton

18 LFD

3rd CAN DIV 101

Calais

BR 50th DIV

Douvres

LONDON

BR 6th PARA DIV

Thames

82nd U

0